Introducing
An Illustrated & Interactive Guide

Introducing Rhetoric
An Illustrated & Interactive Guide

T. Michael W. Halcomb

GlossaHouse
Wilmore, KY
www.GlossaHouse.com

GlossaHouse, LLC
110 Callis Circle
Wilmore, KY 40390

Halcomb, T. Michael W.
 Introducing rhetoric : an illustrated and interactive guide / T. Michael W. Halcomb. – Wilmore, KY : GlossaHouse, ©2018.

       pages : illustrations ; cm.

       Includes bibliographical references.
       ISBN 9781942697664 (paperback)

       1. Rhetoric--Handbooks, manuals, etc.   2. Rhetoric--Textbooks. 3. Rhetoric--Problems, exercises, etc.   4. English language--Composition and exercises.   I. Title.

PN189.H34 2018   808   2018XXXXXX

The fonts used to create this work are available from linguistsoftware.com/lgku.htm. Illustrations & art created by T. Michael W. Halcomb and/or from http://openclipart.org.
Cover Design by T. Michael W. Halcomb
Book Design by T. Michael W. Halcomb

This book is dedicated to Trinity Christian School's Class of 2019.

Table of Contents

Introduction

This book is the fruit of many years of hard and meaningful study. Likewise, it is the result of striving to creatively teach the foundations of ancient rhetoric to a new generation of students and produce a helpful and engaging resource for learners and educators. Indeed, this volume is one I made for use in my own classroom and, as such, have field tested with students.

These particular students are, academically speaking and compared to the national mean, above-average. They are trained in the "Classical Christian" tradition, which places a high premium on the trivium across the curriculum. In their junior and senior years, there is a purposeful focus on ancient rhetoric, which sets the stage for composing a thesis, delivering it before a live audience, and defending it before a respected panel of judges.

Judging by their feedback, *Introducing Rhetoric* is a fun, engaging, and sometimes challenging journey through the core elements of ancient rhetoric and the progymnasmata. In addition to the use of images throughout the first twenty lessons, there is also a lot of humor (I admit, yes, it is often very dry!) alongside many built-in activities. These activities function both to reiterate concepts and provide learners with the opportunity to immediately *do* what they're reading about.

The ways this book could be used in homeschool, high school, college, university, or seminary classrooms is virtually endless. Since the lessons are numbered 1.5, 3.2, 7.4, and so on, one can easily skip around and reorder things if they please. Personally, I work straight through the text each day with students. My strategy is to have them read every single paragraph of the book aloud, taking turns as they do so. When activities are encountered, we pause and complete them. Whatever is not completed may be assigned as homework.

Alongside many of the positive characteristics of this book that I have already mentioned, another that deserves attention is the multicultural nature of the text. Since I have been fortunate enough to have traveled to, studied in, and lived in a number of different cultural contexts, I am able to draw from a wide net of stories, languages, literatures, and personal experiences. I sincerely hope that many of my first-person accounts add a flavor to this volume that I find sorely lacking in many academic works and textbooks. Moreover, while there are some "big words" throughout, I believe I explain them in a down-to-earth manner rather than a dumbed-down one.

Finally, I would like to thank GlossaHouse for accepting this work for publication. Additionally, I want to thank my wife Kristi for her support. A big "Thank you!" also goes out to Trinity Christian School for providing me with the opportunity to teach, an opportunity that has allowed me to create another innovative resource. And once again, I need to thank the students who have read through this book. They discovered typos, errors of other sorts, offered praise and criticism, and all the while, were pretty good interlocutors. Thank you all!

Lent, 2018
T. Michael W. Halcomb

(1.1) What is Rhetoric?

So, here you are, reading a book on rhetoric. Boring, right? Pretty lame, yeah? Maybe. But maybe not. I think you should give it a chance. Why? Because…

…this is a book that can help you.

Umm, how?!

Well, it won't change your looks, but it might just be able to change how you write and speak. Wait, on second thought, maybe it can help change your looks. So, we ask the same thing as our friend above, "Umm, how?!"

So, after the next sentence, stop reading and think for a moment about what you just read. Take a second, look at yourself, and think about what you're wearing.

Finished? Then proceed.

What you're wearing says something about you. Indeed, clothes are like texts—they are meant to be read. What one wears has the ability to convey things about them. Of course, big companies like Nike or Reebok know this. That is precisely why they plaster their logos on things—an act that turns people like you and me into their very own walking billboards.

So, what does that outfit you're wearing right now say about you? (Hopefully, you are wearing an outfit at the moment!) Take a moment and, in the space below, jot down a few thoughts about what message your attire might say about you.

Activity 1: What does your clothing say about you?

Good? Okay, so, you realize that your clothes make a statement. You probably already knew that, at least to some degree. Forrest Gump knew this, too. At one point in the movie bearing his name, he remarked:

"My mama always said you can tell a lot about a person by their shoes, where they're going, where they been…"

Both Forrest and his mama are correct. What they're referring to is precisely what, in a more scholarly sense, many might label "visual rhetoric."

Like words, objects that we see can communicate something to us. Yep, your shoes say something about you. My shirt says something about me. Your friend's hairstyle says something about him or her. These types of things often suggest something or aim to suggest something about a person's personality, mood, social status, etc. In fact, now that you're thinking about it, you might want to change your clothes in order to change the message you're conveying. But wait, you need to finish reading this chapter first!

Mirror, Mirror in my hand, who has the dopest hair in all the land?

In order to get to that point, I want you to look at someone else. If there's no one around in person, look at the photo to the right or a commercial or something similar.

Now, take a moment and, in the space below, jot down a few thoughts about what message their appearance is sending to you.

Activity 2: What does their appearance say about them?

Chances are, the person you looked at was attempting, however subtly or purposefully, to get you to believe something about them.

Or, to put it differently, they were attempting to persuade you to view them a certain way. Yes, even the picture of the guy above, the one who's diverting attention away from his schnoz, is making a fashion statement. Or maybe a non-fashion statement. But that's rhetoric. And despite what you may have heard, rhetoric's not necessarily a bad thing. It's what we do. We are rhetorical beings.

So, Dr. Halcomb, are you saying I'm a rhetorical being? If so, that's totes amazeballs!

Yes, but not as amazeballs as that stache!

Alright, think, for instance, about a police officer or an athlete. Seriously though, stop looking at that dude's stache and focus! Cops and athletes, they have a look. And their look, their clothing aims to persuade you about their identity. A police officer's uniform, for instance, seeks to persuade you that he or she is an authority figure. An athlete's uniform typically seeks to persuade you that he or she is an individual who is part of a team. These are social signals that reinforce common messages and ideals.

When I was in high school, I played on a soccer team and the coach made us look after our own jerseys. We were responsible for keeping them, washing them, and bringing them to each game. If we happened to leave our uniforms at home, there was no chance of playing; we had to sit out. Why? Because wearing street clothes while playing in the game would confuse people and persuasively send the message that our team was clueless about how to conduct themselves during a match. That's not something he wanted to persuade fans, opponents, officials, or the league of.

In a similar way, the words we choose to use send a message about who we are, what we value, where we're from, and what our social standing might be. When we open our mouths, much of the time we do so with the intent to persuade others of something. That's precisely what rhetoric is—the art of persuasion. And this art form is pretty much always in play everywhere by everyone.

In the next few chapters, we'll consider the study of the origins and development of this near-omnipresent aspect of our lives. For now, however, have a look around you again. Find two bits of text nearby and discuss how they are attempting to persuade you.

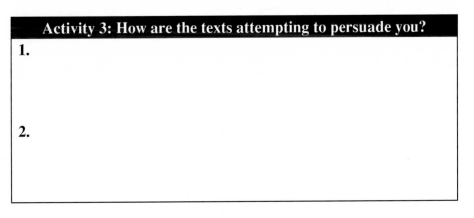

Activity 3: How are the texts attempting to persuade you?

1.

2.

(1.2) Rhetoric in Antiquity

Many books on rhetoric start with the Greeks. I get that, I do. I sincerely love the ancient Greek language and also studying that timeframe within the scope of world history. But, regardless of what others might say, the reality is this: rhetoric existed prior to the Greeks. True story! If people were writing, talking, and wearing clothes, you can be sure rhetoric was present. And, indeed, it was.

Since this is the case, and since we want a fuller picture of rhetoric in the ancient world, it will be beneficial to consider the role of rhetoric in a number of different cultures located throughout the Mediterranean basin. But you might be thinking: Why even concern ourselves with this ancient stuff anyway?

Well, I could provide many responses to that but I think one of the best is that it gives us a chance to imagine—imagine other people and what happened in their lives. That, in itself, is an act that teaches us to be focused on more than just ourselves. Even so, one excellent result of that has to do with the fact that when we learn about how others lived and talked, we can think more clearly about how we should live and talk, how we should do rhetoric.

Keeping that in mind, let's think briefly about rhetoric among ancient Semitic, Egyptian, and Greco-Roman people. But before we do, I'm going to go ahead and ask you to prepare yourself with a little imagining activity. You may know nothing about these people or their contexts and that's okay. At least wager a guess with regard to the following question: What do you think some of the settings were where rhetoric was used in antiquity? Aim for three responses.

Activity 1: In what settings was rhetoric used in antiquity?
1.
2.
3.

I, of course, can't read your answers. Too bad! Maybe someday. I'm sure, however, that given the size of that brain of yours, they were impressive. Now, keep using your thinker to trek with me. I want you to consider the ancient Hebrew people in relation to rhetoric. As you might know, these folks were called Israelites early on and much later Jews. They were also called "Semites" and, so, things related to them are often described as "Semitic."

The Hebrew people are subjects of the Old Testament, which was first written in Hebrew and contained a small bit of Aramaic. They are also responsible for composing, compiling, and preserving the Old Testament. In the Old Testament there is…wait for it…rhetoric. Since Hebrew precedes Greek, and since rhetoric is present in Hebrew literature, we can conclude that rhetoric was alive and well prior to Greek.

Moi, Moses, the founder of rhetoric? *Tov maod*!

Some have even attempted to argue that Moses was the founder of rhetoric. Whether that is the case, we may never really know. Others have drawn attention to the Hebrew orator, Isaiah.

One researcher, Yehoshua Gitay, has argued that the *dispositio* of Isa 44:24-45:13, which precedes the origins of Greek rhetoric, contains many of the elements the Greeks would later assign labels to. For instance, he asserts the following outline: Isa 44:24-28 (*exordium*); 45:1-7 (*narratio*); 45:8 (*confirmatio*); and 45:9-13 (*peroratio*).[1] Gitay also shows how the notions later defined as

---

[1] Yehoshua Gitay, "Rhetorical Analysis of Isaiah 40-48: A Study of the Art of Prophetic Persuasion" (Ph.D. diss., Emory University, 1978), 324-47.

logos, *pathos*, and *ethos* are at work in this text. (If those terms are truly foreign to you, relax—you'll learn more about them in later chapters.)

For me, whether or not the Hebrews, Egyptians, or Greeks are the originators of rhetoric is really beside the point here. What is significant, however, is understanding the fact that rhetoric was present among each of these groups. So, what you should do now is find a Bible and read Isa 44:24-45:13.

Once you have done that, take note of at least two things you find interesting with regard to rhetoric. For example, you could note the repetition of verbs and very short sentences and what the intended effect of this might have been on readers and/or listeners. Oh, wait, now that I've pointed that one out, you can't use it. #SorryNotSorry! As I said before, you're probably pretty smart. So, come up with your own answers.

Activity 2: What do you find interesting about Isaiah's rhetoric?

1.

2.

In our overview of ancient Semitic rhetoric, we saw that Moses was often lifted up as its creator. Despite the fact that Moses was raised in Egypt, he is not viewed as the father of ancient Egyptian—and thus African—rhetoric. Instead, that honor goes to Ptahhotep. What a name, eh!?

Ptahhotep was an early city official under the reign of King Izezi (also Isesi or Isosi or whatever you find to be the most fun way to say it). Izezi ruled during what is known as the 5th Dynasty of the Old Kingdom (ca. 2380-2342 BCE). In a work titled *The Instruction of Ptahhotep*, which is dated to around 2160 BCE (6th Dynasty), there are thirty-seven maxims or sayings.

These sayings are sandwiched between a prologue and epilogue. They deal with speech, morals, and governance. Perhaps, more importantly, these teachings were composed by a father for his son. Moreover, they often share similarities with the Wisdom Literature of the Old Testament and Apocrypha.

Ptahhotep has lots to say about speech and rhetoric. He himself refers to his teachings as "the formulations of excellent discourse." He claims that his hope is that these teachings will function as "the standard of excellent discourse" and bring "profit for him who will hear." Kind of reminds of us of that whole Jesus bit about having "ears to hear" doesn't it?

Ptahhotep's first maxim concludes with, "Fair speech is rarer than the emerald." The second, set in the context of a dispute, commands speakers to "Make little of evil speech" and, along with the third and fourth, places a high premium on silence toward an opponent rather than rebuke or rebuttal. Thus, not only is speech itself important but good and proper speech are of great significance.

The sixth maxim warns against speaking too highly of oneself and the seventh about proper discourse as a guest during mealtime. Here, the instruction is: "Don't speak to him [the host] until he summons" because "One does not know what may displease." Instead, he suggests: "Speak when he (the host) has addressed you, then your words will please the heart." The eighth maxim warns against the use of reviling speech and malignity. Admonitions to silence and warnings against boasting and/or vain speech can be found in maxims nine, twelve, and fourteen.

I could continue with many more examples from this and other pieces of Egyptian literature but these suffice. You get the point from the work of Ptahhotep alone: rhetoric was present and in use in ancient Egypt. This, of course, is not to take anything away from the Greeks. It is, though, an attempt to a) correct some misunderstanding about rhetoric prior to the Greeks, and b) to show that rhetoric was all around the ancient Mediterranean very early on.

Alright, now that you have some knowledge on Egyptian rhetoric under your belt (what an odd saying, huh!), it's time for a brief thought experiment. Imagine that you received an invitation from Ptahhotep to add one of your own, original, and rhetorically killer sayings to his. Let's say, oh, one about rhetoric at dinner. What would you add? Remember, this will live on forever, so, make it good!

Activity 3: Create an original mealtime maxim for Ptahhotep

Okay, let's switch gears a bit. Time to talk about the Greeks. The contribution of the ancient Greeks is definitely important in any discussion of rhetoric. Because of that, a little background information is needed.

A number of events in antiquity led to the development and understanding of rhetoric as an art form. The urbanization of cities such as Athens in 8th-7th centuries BCE was a major factor. Likewise, the transition from an oral culture in the 5th century to an oral *and* literary culture played an important role. An increased interest in the 4th century of democracy and civil law, as well as the desire for freedom of expression under the reign of Alexander the Great, also factored into the rise of rhetoric in Hellenistic culture.

One specific event, though, is often appealed to as a possible point of origin: the expulsion of the Theron dynasty tyrants at Agrigentum, Sicily. This is believed by some to have necessitated the use of rhetoric to defend oneself and one's property. Against this, however, some argue that the development of rhetoric finds its origins in Homer. The researcher Samuel Ijsseling, for example, has said:

"Among the ancients, Homer is most often considered to be the father of rhetoric, with nearly half of the Iliad and more than two thirds of the *Odyssey* consisting of speeches by actors. Here one can find the practical application of almost all rhetorical rules and directives which only later were explicitly formulated."

In fact, it has been noted that, in his work titled *On Rhetoric*, there are nearly forty references to and quotes from Homer made by Aristotle. In *Iliad* 9:443, Homer's awareness of rhetoric may be acknowledged in his comment that Achilles's father, Peleus, calls him to travel to see the wars in order that he might "be a speaker (rhetor) of words and doer of deeds." In *Odyssey* 8:167-173, Homer notes that it is the gods who give certain men "eloquence," and who may "crown him with words, that in him they (listeners) will notice delight." Such a person will be "steadfast in his speaking," which is "soothing" and brings about "reverence."

Yet, George Kennedy, one of the great rhetorical scholars of our time, questions whether these and other references are enough to assert that Homer can be identified as the founder or father of rhetoric. He correctly, I believe, answers in the negative.[2]

It is likely closer to the fact that, while Aristotle drew on Homer, he did so not with the understanding that Homer was the founder or father of rhetoric as an art or science, but rather as a historian and storyteller whose works he admired. As the scholar Todd Frobish comments, "Homer seems a useful starting point" for "understanding the genealogy of character as a factor in persuasion."[3] Like Homer, the 5th century Sophist, Empedocles, has also been labeled the "father of rhetoric." Aristotle, as well as Diogenes Laertius citing Aristotle, both mention this.

"Aristotle, in his *Sophist*, says Empedocles was the first to find rhetoric, as Zeno was dialectic."
-Diogenes Laertius, *Empedocles*

"Yep, my boy D. is mos def right. I said that."
-Aristotle, *Never*

---

[2] This is asserted in Brian Vickers, *Classical Rhetoric in English Poetry: With a New Preface and Annotated Bibliography* (Carbondale, Southern Illinois University Press, 1989), 16.

[3] Todd S. Frobish, "An Origin of a Theory: A Comparison of Ethos in the Homeric *Iliad* with that Found in Aristotle's *Rhetoric*," *Rhetoric Review* 22/1 (2003): 29.

Those would make great family photos wouldn't they!? Now, back to the lecture at hand. The famous orator, Quintilian, in *Institutio Oratoria* 3.1.8, makes a similar statement. He says, "For the first one, after the poets, who is said to have moved in the direction of rhetoric, is Empedocles."

Given that we have no extant writings of Empedocles, it is difficult to arrive at a single conclusion as to why he was described as the first rhetor. Thanks, history!

One factor which lends some credence to this idea is that Empedocles was the teacher of the revered orator Gorgias. Along with Empedocles, Corax and his student Tisias, are all believed to have been natives of Sicily. Not surprisingly, then, Corax and Tisias have also been identified with the beginnings of rhetoric (Cicero, *de Orat.* 1.20.91; *Brut.* 12.46). Leading proponents in the school for rhetoric at Syracuse, they both wrote treatises on rhetoric.

It may well have been the case, then, that Gorgias was a student of Tisias. Yet, it is Tisias to whom Cicero points his focus. Cicero describes him as the founder (*inventore*; see: *de Orat.* 1.20.91). As noted above, it is Cicero who addressed the need for eloquence in speaking that arose from the onslaught of private lawsuits after the expulsion of the tyrants in Sicily (*Brut.* 12.46). In the school of Corax and Tisias, rhetoric was defined as "the art of persuasion." That, of course, is the definition I follow here.

Since Greek is such a huge part of the history of rhetoric, and since most of the terminology used still today comes from ancient Greek, we'll read more about it in future chapters. Thus, as we approach our stopping point here, finish up with one last activity. Even if you don't believe it, give a short answer as to why you think it "might" be possible that Greek rhetoric developed in Sicily.

Activity 4: 1 reason Greek rhetoric may have started in Sicily

(1.3) Rhetoric in Modernity

The study of rhetoric in modernity, that is, the twenty-first century, finds itself situated under the umbrella of Communication Studies (CS). Really, much of this began in the 1950s and 60s with works by authors such as Robert Cathcart, Anthony Hillbruner, Stephen Toulmin, and Chaïm Perelman and Lucie Olbrechts-Tyteca.

In these studies, the focus was largely on the art and teaching of public speaking. Rooted in the ancient classical tradition, they drew from revered authors like Aristotle, Cicero, and Quintilian. Appealing to these authors helped give the discipline of rhetoric, which they were attempting to popularize, some academic credibility and pedigree.

CS became increasingly relevant as technology made advances. Alongside this, progress in other scientific fields, such linguistics and philosophy, was being used to lend additional credence to CS. It was in this context, especially with the rise of structuralism in the 1970s and 80s, that the resurrection of Rhetorical Criticism (RC) came about.

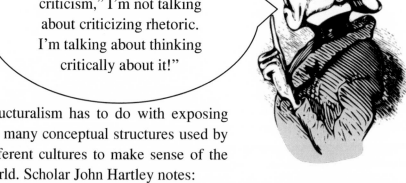

Bear in mind, boys and girls, that when I say "rhetorical criticism," I'm not talking about criticizing rhetoric. I'm talking about thinking critically about it!"

Structuralism has to do with exposing the many conceptual structures used by different cultures to make sense of the world. Scholar John Hartley notes:

"Since structuralism began to disclose how much of what we know and experience is structured by the sign systems we inhabit and

14

encounter, there has been a noticeable revival in rhetoric."[4] Thus, there is much to the relationship between structuralism and rhetoric.

Researchers Alan Gross and William Keith point out, however, that the contrasts between the two traditions are quite significant. They argue that "The rhetorical tradition, typically with its eye on the political orator, has emphasized adaptation and function, while the structuralist tradition—from Marx, to Lévi-Strauss, to Lukas and Goldman, Gramsci and Foucault—has emphasized how larger social-cultural structures determine the possibilities for individual speakers."[5] They continue:

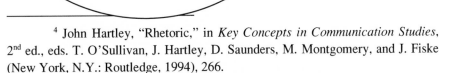

"In the first tradition (which Gaonkar calls the 'Aristotelian ideology' and 'the inventional strategy' of reading), speakers are the origin of meaning, adapting their words to their audiences and purposes.

"In the second tradition, the speaker is merely the point of articulation, where the macro-structures of culture and society…give the illusion of individual choice, and hegemonically constrain the choice of speakers, who cannot 'adapt' what they do not control."

---

[4] John Hartley, "Rhetoric," in *Key Concepts in Communication Studies*, 2nd ed., eds. T. O'Sullivan, J. Hartley, D. Saunders, M. Montgomery, and J. Fiske (New York, N.Y.: Routledge, 1994), 266.

[5] Alan G. Gross and William M. Keith, *Rhetorical Hermeneutics: Invention and Interpretation in the Age of Science* (Albany, N.Y.: State University of New York Press, 1997), 226.

From this, we gather that much of the question has to do with the orator's interaction with society. Which one is the central point of influence upon the other? Some would contend that, whereas structuralism has as its aim to divide culture into discrete units, "rhetorical theory carves up language into its various units."[6]

Thus, there is something of a "genealogical resemblance between rhetoric and the structural analysis of culture." This is much of what "set the stage for the study of rhetoric as an anatomy of ancient language and the culture of which that language is an expression."[7] Or, to put it differently: every time you speak, not only does *the way* you speak say something about you, *what* you say does, too. In fact, it says something more than just about you—it says a lot about your culture and society, too.

Think of the most recent "new word" you've heard. When spoken, what does it say about both the speaker and their culture? Give an explanation in 3 or 4 sentences.

Activity 1: What does the word say about the speaker & culture?

---

[6] Ibid.
[7] Ibid.

(1.4) The Rhetorical Situation, Pt. 1

Have you ever wondered why young people tend to speak differently than those who are older? Like, why young people say "like" all the time? And like, why older people really, like, don't? We linguists refer to this way of using "like" as "Quotative Like." All that means is that it's a way to introduce something someone says/is saying or even thinks/is thinking.

And I was like, "Oh! My! Goodness!" And she was like, "Girl, you best step off!"

For reals? She was like, "Step off!"? Omg! I can't even. I so wonder what's wrong with her? Like, Ugh!

Remember the previous lesson that talked about how your clothes and others' clothes make statements, how they say things? Well, so does *how* you talk. And so does *what* you say. If you can think of those things as part of say, a specific occasion, then it isn't difficult to understand the concept referred to as the "rhetorical situation."

If we break down the term "rhetorical situation," we find that it actually consists of a number of important elements. In my view, there are seven specific aspects to every rhetorical situation and, in the remainder of this lesson, as well as the next handful of lessons, we'll look at each of those in turn. It is imperative to keep in mind, though, that these elements are all connected. That is, by virtue of being together rather than separate, they form the rhetorical situation—the context.

The Speaker

Alright, roll with me here. When I say speaker, I need you to know that I do not only mean someone who is speaking. That's not too difficult to understand, right!? For instance, when you are reading a book, the author is typically not literally standing before you speaking the words on the page. Even so, he's still the one saying what's being said, he's the speaker.

So, if someone's a speaker, that doesn't mean they're always speaking aloud. It just means that they're the one, somehow and in some way, making a statement. Maybe with audible words or printed words or body language, etc. Okay, good? Good!

When you finish reading this paragraph, go ahead and look at the triangle below. Inside this one big triangle are seven smaller triangles. The big triangle *represents* the rhetorical situation as a whole. The seven smaller bits *constitute* each element of the rhetorical situation/context. The speaker, that is, the one with something to say, is but one of those elements. There are more!

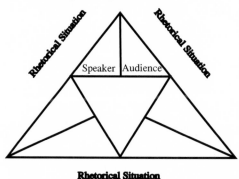

As we continue learning about the rhetorical triangle, the remaining slots will be filled in. Actually, you see that a second triangle already has a label, namely, the one titled "Audience." Since you now see that, this seems like a great place to talk about it.

More than likely, you already have some understanding of how a Speaker and an Audience fit together. Keep reading and see if, indeed, that's the case.

The Audience

Without an audience, a speaker isn't really important. Without an audience, a speaker's words have little significance. Thus, every speaker needs an audience. Similarly, if an audience showed up to a venue and no one was there to speak, they'd find it pretty pointless to be sitting there. So, there is actually a mutual need: a speaker needs an audience just as much as an audience needs a speaker.

As a public speaker, I have been in rooms that were packed with hundreds of people listening. At other times, however, such as at very small conferences, I've been in a room with only two other people (both of whom were forced to be there to preside over the session). Not having a decent-sized audience was totally lame.

One time during my college years, when I was part of a musical duo, my friend and I secured a show in small town in Indiana. It was at a fairly well-known coffee shop on the circuit so we drove hours to get there. After we set up and were ready to play, literally, not a soul showed up. Even the barista and waitresses didn't stick around to listen—they went into the break room. Again, lame! Not having an audience is about as fun as getting a TSA pat down.

A speaker, as you know, sends a message. An audience receives that message, interprets it, and assigns it meaning. Thus, two vital elements to a rhetorical situation, that is, the context of what's happening, are a speaker and an audience. As we press on, I trust you'll bear these things in mind and continue to consider their importance in relation to the other elements of the rhetorical triangle. (And, no, I didn't play in a harp and flute band. Just in case, you know, you were wondering or anything.)

(1.5) The Rhetorical Situation, Pt. 2

You thought I forgot didn't you? You know, about including any activities in the previous lesson. Nope. I didn't forget. Just consider me gracious and kind and awesome and cool and generous. Okay, enough. Otherwise, I'll start to think you're trying to be a brown nose.

Speaking of nose, do you smell that? Yeah? It's the smell of an activity. Woohoo! Let's see how well your memory is. In the box below, write some short definitions for the following terms: rhetorical situation, speaker, and audience. Go.

Activity 1: Provide definitions / descriptions for the terms below
1. Rhetorical Situation:
2. Speaker:
3. Audience:

As you should already know, a speaker and audience are simply two components of the rhetorical triangle, that is, the rhetorical situation or context. There are, of course, more. Let's not waste any time. Let's go ahead and add an element to the rhetorical triangle.

The Purpose

The backbone and centerpiece of the rhetorical triangle is the purpose. You might be surprised to realize that the purpose is more than just the reason the speaker is speaking. It is that, to be sure. Yet, it is more. It is also *the reason*, for instance, that the audience is gathering. Moreover, it has to do with *why* something is being spoken and listened to, *where* all this is taking place, *when* it is

20

happening, and *how* it is being delivered. We'll talk about that last point in just a moment. For now, however, let's focus on the other stuff.

Have you ever noticed how, during presidential campaigns, candidates try very hard to blend in with the people they're speaking to? For instance, on the campaign trail, many politicians go to places like a local power plant where many blue-collar workers can be found. *The reason* they might go there is to criticize the current administration's stance on power and offer an alternative. *Why* would they say such things and *why* would people listen? Because, at the very least, the people have a stake in this matter and the candidate knows it.

The candidate also tries to earn brownie points with the audience by going to them. This may inadvertently earn him or her points with onlookers, too, as they come off as a normal, hardworking, down-to-earth, and relatable person. That's why these campaign speeches happen *where* they do.

It's also why they happen *when* they do! They often take place in the middle of the day or just at the end of the work day. This is never accidental. Maybe the workers were given a short break to come listen, paid for in coverage by the candidate. Or maybe they can be applauded for all the effort they put in after their 9-to-5 finished that day. It's planned out and strategic. Together, these things make the purpose of any speech discernable.

The Medium

Along with the previous point, as you will see in the rhetorical triangle below, medium has now been added. The medium is basically the means by which the speech is delivered. Is it spoken? If so, is it read with or without a microphone? Is it memorized or spontaneous? The medium has to do with *how* it's being delivered.

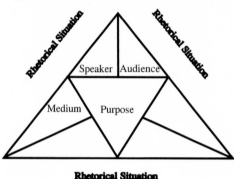

Rhetorical Situation

Or, is the message coming via print, as in a book or newspaper? Maybe it's something being aired on the radio or television. Or perhaps in the case of, say, the President, it's coming from staff members instead of him or her directly.

The means by which the message comes is incredibly important. In fact, there's an old saying that asserts "The medium is the message." In the activity below, describe why, on the one hand, the medium and the message can be so easily confused. On the other hand, describe why it may be fallacious to confuse them.

Activity 2: Discuss the link between the medium and the message
1. The medium:
2. The message:

(2.1) The Rhetorical Situation, Pt. 3

Ain't no party like a Chapter 2 party 'cause Chapter 2 party don't stop. Yeah! Well, actually, chapter 2 will come to an end but before that can happen we have to get going. So, in the words of Matthew McConaughey, "Alright! Alright! Alright!" Let's get this party started!

As with everything else in this book, the concern is rhetoric—the art of persuasion. To complete our rhetorical triangle, we must consider the three modes of persuasion that the ancient Greeks and Romans discussed: ethos, logos, and pathos. These ancient ideals have had an immense staying force since their inception in antiquity.

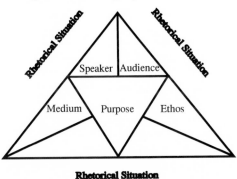

Rhetorical Situation

It was Aristotle who referred to this triad of modes as "appeals." It is worth noting that, whether to a greater or lesser degree, every argument that someone makes uses all three of these appeals. Moreover, each of these appeals has different effects.

When it comes to ethos, what is really in view is the reputation of the speaker. This includes items like the speaker's credentials and relevant experience. As a speaker, there have been many times when, before giving a talk, someone will go up before me and tell the audience about many of my accomplishments. There have been occasions, too, where that act was preceded by a brochure or pamphlet printed with similar details.

Such an act is a means of helping establish my credibility before I even step in front of anyone. It's a way of enacting the saying "his credibility precedes him." The hope is that this will not only prime the audience for listening but also help immediately build rapport between me, the speaker, and them, the audience.

One thing that interests me about the whole, let's-announce-the-speaker's-credentials thing, is that if the speaker were to stand up and introduce himself or herself that way, it would end up damaging their credibility. Why? Because it would come off as bragging and as an act of arrogance.

There are other aspects, too, that help or hurt a speaker's credibility: appearance, sound, mannerisms, nerves, lack of preparation, etc. In short, ethos has to do with one's persona and, truth be told, we're all always working on our personas (or: *personae*, if you want the correct Latin ending). See what I did there? I dropped in some Latin in an attempt to spice up what I said. People use foreignisms all the time, dropping them into English, often with the hope of appearing smart—polishing up their personas.

Every time you speak, you're working on your persona, emitting signals to your audience telling them how to read you. Think of yourself as one of those fancy, trick sign-holders out in front of a store or sale. They stand there and spin signs, flip signs, throw signs up into the air and catch them, etc.

They're trying to capture your attention in order to tell you something about them, something like, "Hey, I'm affiliated with this store." I'm like them and you're like them; our ethos is always telling the people looking at us what we're about.

Take a moment and do an internet search for the phrase "Basketball Player Deodorant Commercial." In the space below, describe the person in your ad and explain how ethos is at work (or at least trying to be at work).

Activity 1: Discuss the presence of ethos in a video ad

(2.2) The Rhetorical Situation, Pt. 4

"Hey! Psst. Hey! Right here, Mister. Are you the fella who wants to know about the topic of this chapter?" *<looks left, then right, then straight>* See that guy to my left, the one reading? He's almost finished already and he tells me it's about pathos. Yeah, pathos. That's what it's about. Mums the word ya' filthy animal!"

As the man said, this chapter is, indeed, about pathos. And as you see below, it is the next element to add to our rhetorical triangle. Like ethos, which comes from the Greek term ἔθος (eh-thōs) and has to do with one's visible customs or habits, one's persona, pathos also comes from a Greek word, namely, πάθος (pah-thōs). This meaning of this word, however, has to do with emotion and passion.

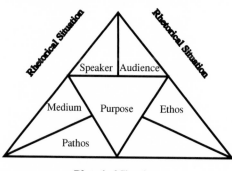

Rhetorical Situation

In fact, the English word "passion" comes directly from this Greek term. How? Well, through Latin. In Latin, the verb form is *patio*. I trust you can see the resemblance between *pathos* and *patio*, yeah? Great. The fourth principal part of the verb in Latin takes the form of the perfect passive participle: *passus*. See the connection? This is precisely where phrases like "The 'passion' of the Christ" derive.

Thus, passion has to do with, at some level, suffering, which is itself an experience of intense emotion. Within the context of ancient rhetoric, it was also connected to emotion—mainly having an emotional speaking style. This style, in turn, would tug at the heart strings of the audience. A good orator can play on pathos to make a crowd happy or sad or angry, etc. In short, pathos can be used to move the audience to a desired state and to pursue a course of action.

If you've ever listened to a speech of Martin Luther King, Jr., then you've witnessed pathos at work. King was a master orator and one of the greatest, if not *the* greatest, speaker in American history. He knew how to employ pathos perfectly. His powerful voice and eloquent speech were infused with pathos.

In fact, once you finish reading this paragraph, I would like you to search the web for "Martin Luther King, Jr., Dream Speech." Watch at least five minutes of the event and return here to write about it. In particular, write about how a) King's speech demonstrates pathos, and b) whether the audience seems to be moved by the experience of the delivery of the speech and, if so, how you know. In addition, write about how c) you were or were not moved.

Activity 1: Discuss the presence of pathos in King's speech
a)
b)
c)

(2.3) The Rhetorical Situation, Pt. 5

We have reached the third and final appeal, which also happens to be the last element in our rhetorical triangle: logos. No, this does not mean logos, like decals or small icons or symbols restaurants use to distinguish themselves. That's a different word and, in fact, the "s" on the end is even pronounced differently. Don't believe me? Say both words aloud!

Anyway, you can see that logos has been added to our recurring image below. In the ancient world, the term 'logos' had a wide range of meanings. It could refer to a rumor, word, a speech, speech in general, an explanation, a story, and is even a term applied to Jesus in the Gospel of John that functions somewhat like a name. You've probably heard Jn 1:1 before: "In the beginning was the [logos] word."

Context is key in discerning it's meaning. When it comes to ancient rhetoric, for instance, logos could refer to a reasoned argument or speech, especially one with eloquence. This focus on argument is telling. It suggests to us that, rather than be heavy on the emotive side like pathos or weighty on appearances like ethos, it is more concerned with using language to make people think.

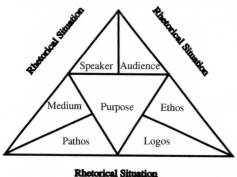

Because of this, some attempt to connect logos with logic proper, that is, the field of logic. That works, but only to a degree. If, instead, one thinks of logic in terms of deductive and inductive logic or reasoning, that's closer to the mark.

The point is this: logos is meant to lead listeners and readers to consider things like evidence, proofs, arguments, etc. It is, we might say, more of an appeal to the mind. It is more cerebral. Logos is often at work when testimonies, statistics, quotes, riddles, and jokes are used. The goal is to get people thinking.

When I was a mere lad, six-years old to be precise, I actually remember sitting in a first-grade classroom in Ohio watching the launch of the Challenger space shuttle. Only a few seconds after takeoff, it blew up. I didn't quite grasp what had happened but I knew it wasn't good, especially by the way the teacher reacted.

Now, I wasn't into speeches at that time in my life and I couldn't have told a good speech from a bad one. But I can today. At the time, Ronald Reagan was President of the United States. He gave a speech that evening and, as you might imagine, it was laden with pathos. No, not in a manipulative way, but in a good, caring, and responsible way. And it also had portions of logos.

One section that stands out to me is this bit: "We've grown used to wonders in this century. It's hard to dazzle us. But for 25 years the United States space program has been doing just that. We've grown used to the idea of space, and perhaps we forget that we've only just begun. We're still pioneers. They, the members of the Challenger crew, were pioneers."

After taking a moment to reflect on these words, in the space below, identify where logos is present. Further, discuss how this small section of Reagan's talk was meant to get people thinking, that is, to be thought-provoking.

Activity 1: Discuss the presence of logos in Reagan's speech

(2.4) The Rhetorical Situation, Pt. 6

Go ahead, you can thank me. Go on. Say it. Friend, I sincerely appreciate that; I'm glad I could help. Oh, wondering what you're thanking me for? A short chapter! You're welcome.

All I really want to do is review eight of the terms you have been thinking about recently and add one. That's it. And just to make it easier, I'll start with the new one we need to consider: exigency. Really, that's just a fancy word meaning "what's needed." In any given rhetorical situation, what's needed is a problem or issue, some sort of obstacle.

"Come Watson, come…The game is afoot. I've discovered exigency."

Without a problem, without exigency, there's not much to speak about. Stated differently, if there's no underlying exigency, then there can be no purpose. And if there's no purpose, then there is really no rhetorical situation.

It is as if exigency is the root system underlying purpose; we don't see it on the surface of our rhetorical triangle but it's definitely there underneath. I trust you can grasp this simple concept. Now, let's move on. After each of the terms below, write a brief definition. Then, you'll be finished with this lesson. And since you offered me a "Thank you" ahead of time, let me say, "Well done" ahead of time.

1. **Rhetorical Situation:**
2. **Speaker:**
3. **Audience:**
4. **Medium:**
5. **Purpose:**
6. **Ethos:**
7. **Pathos:**
8. **Logos:**
9. **Exigency:**

(2.5) Stasis Theory

Over the last several years I have become convinced of a few points with regard to social media: 1) Facebook is the place where good conversation goes to die; 2) YouTube is the place where encouragement goes to die; and, 3) Twitter is the place where good grammar and diction go to die. Since I use all three, I suppose you could say part of me has died.

My point is this: social media may be convenient but it is limiting in how we can express ourselves to and with one another. If your kneejerk reaction is to challenge that claim, I'm going to go ahead and channel my inner Dwight Schrute and offer this rejoinder: "False!"

The first several years of using a platform like Facebook, I was an idiot. I wasted so much of my life arguing with people on there and never really accomplished anything by it. It was largely pointless and fruitless. I chalk most of that up to one thing: people not achieving stasis.

Yes, that sounds kind of fancy but all it really means is that people are talking past one another; they think they're arguing about something but, in all reality, they're arguing about two different things. When that happens, in terms of rhetoric, we might say they are out of stasis or that stasis has not been reached.

In ancient oratory, stasis played on the image of two people in conversation facing one another. That is, they were standing face-to-face and in alignment. That alignment helped them talk to one another and stay on topic. Now, imagine if the two people talking were to each take a step, one to the left and one to the right. At this point, they're no longer looking at each other but past each other. If they start talking, they're talking past one another.

This is precisely what happens on social media. Since people are not face to face, they fail to reach stasis and, instead, talk past one another. Sometimes, okay most of the time, that talking past devolves to name-calling, put-downs, false accusations, smearing, etc. And that's why I stand by my claim that Facebook is a place where good conversation goes to die.

We've all seen this. Right now, for example, some people are losing their minds about NFL players not standing during the National Anthem. Others are just as vehement in their conviction that this is a free country and nobody should be forced to act against their convictions. It all started when Colin Kaepernick, a black quarterback for the San Francisco 49ers, was the first to kneel. He did this at a time when he felt the frequent attacks from police officers on unarmed black men stood contrary to what the flag they swore allegiance to represented.

The issue wasn't at all about the flag; it was about the persistent unfair treatment of black men by government officials. It was a race issue, not a flag issue. Yet, many in failing to recognize that, continue to lodge false accusations, curse, put down, and shame him (and those siding with him) by claiming he is disrespecting the flag. Thus, this is one example of stasis not being reached; Kaepernick and his naysayers are out of stasis.

There are ways, however, that the situation could be clarified and rectified and that stasis could be reached. Well, probably not on Facebook or social media but in person. The means of doing this is asking several different types of questions (see below) about the arguments and claims being made by a person.

1) Is a claim of fact, that is, whether something exists or happened, being made?
2) Is a claim of definition, namely, how something is or should be defined, being made?
3) Is a claim of quality, how good or bad something is, being made?
4) Is a claim of cause/effect, how something started and/or its resulting effects being made?
5) Is a claim of proposal, that is, the best proposed course of action, being made?

Let's apply this, not to Kaepernick himself, but to someone arguing that Kaepernick is unpatriotic and, therefore, unworthy to be an American. (Yes, these people exist!) Considering our list of five questions, we could ask each of them in order to achieve stasis with this individual:

1) What are the facts about and/or reasons why Kaepernick took a knee during the anthem?
2) Do you think it's possible that the meaning of Kaepernick's kneeling has been misunderstood?
   a. Do you know of any other acts that you would classify as unpatriotic?
   b. How is this similar to or different than those acts?
3) Is kneeling, which is a form of silent protest, a positive or negative thing? Why?
   a. Is this form of protest better or worse than other forms?
4) What caused Kaepernick to kneel in protest?
   a. What are some of the resultant effects of his kneeling?
5) Would it be beneficial to consider whether required and specific forms of posture during the National Anthem might need to change?

In the space below, write about a time when you witnessed or participated in a discussion or argument lacking stasis. What was the issue they thought they were arguing about but, in fact, were not? How did it end?

Activity 1: Describe an exchange you witnessed that lacked stasis

(3.1) Invention

When I was a teenager, there was a fun show on television titled "Whose Line is it Anyway?" The premise of the show was to put four impromptu actors on a stage, give them an unexpected prompt, and challenge them to come up with a creative act. Most of the time, they excelled at this and the result was a hilarious skit.

For most people, the thought of stepping in front of a crowd is terrifying enough. Adding television cameras would only make it worse. And incorporating the element of the unknown on top of that would simply be paralyzing. Yet, these actors had mastered it, which was quite impressive. (And no, they didn't do it by imagining the audience in their underwear! Talk about paralyzing!)

Really, what they had mastered was the rhetorical art of invention (Latin: *inventio*)—finding something to say. How did they do it? Well, beyond sheer creativity and lots of practice, they drew on common categories of material. It was as if a mental storehouse of topics existed that orators could draw from in order to come up with something to say. Thus, they are not inventing things out of thin air, but summoning knowledge from a place or places already known and familiar. Thus, a speaker engaging in "inventing" is engaging in remembering, calling to the fore of the mind things already stored in the back of it.

"A Student without talent will find my work as about as profitable as bad soil finds a lecture on farming."
-Quintilian

This was something that Jesus often did. In recognizing his audiences, he often drew from a stock of parables, maxims, proverbs, and teachings that they could relate to. Some of the topics were ceremonial in nature, others judicial, and others vocational. Speakers like Aristotle, Quintilian, and Cicero did the same thing.

Stasis is a common rhetorical and performative technique that has been around for and persisted through the ages. Importantly, stasis is required for invention to work. A good speaker will be aware of the issue at hand and get on the same page as the audience. He or she will aim to move the audience from their current position to a different one, even if that difference is only slight. If a speaker cannot find something to say, he or she will speak past the audience (i.e. not be in stasis) or flounder and not say anything at all.

Finally, it is worth noting that invention is the first of what is known as the 5 Canons of Rhetoric. (By the way, the word canon here should not be confused with cannon!) Canon comes from an ancient Greek term meaning "rule" or "standard." Thus, these are the 5 standards used in devising a speech from its inception to its delivery. They are meant to aid orators in their persuasive efforts. We will look at the remaining four in subsequent chapters. Got it? Blink once if 'yes,' and twice if 'no.' I didn't see that so I'll assume you blinked once.

Now, don't blink (see what I did there?) because it's time to write. In the space below, after finding an example where Jesus may be engaging in invention, discuss how and why you believe that might be the case.

Activity 1: Describe an instance where Jesus uses invention

(3.2) Arrangement

Moving is never fun. Packing everything, loading everything, unpacking everything, and rearranging everything has a way of sucking the life out of you. On top of all that, adjusting to new people and a new place is often a challenge. The last time we moved, one of the things I found most irritating was not really knowing where I was going.

To make matters more complicated, road work was taking place and, on a very frequent basis, streets were completely blocked off and inaccessible. Thus, I had to find an alternate route, a detour. The thing is, there were no detour signs telling me what to do. The city just assumed that either a) I knew where to go, or b) I would rely on technology to tell me. But (a) wasn't true at all and (b) was problematic for a number or reasons (e.g. didn't bring a phone, didn't have a data plan, didn't have a GPS device, didn't like tinkering with technology while driving, etc.).

"So, how's the GPS on this thing?"

"Good! But the install cost me some big *bucks*."

For me, it's just no fun driving in a new-to-me town widely under construction with no signage to help guide the way. Signs would have been super helpful and would have made navigating the streets much easier. Fact: Signs matter. In a similar way, how one structures a speech, talk, or paper matters. The structure of a speech should consist of a number of signs or signals to help those being addressed navigate what is said. With regard to rhetoric, this is what the ancient Romans referred to as a *dispositio*, what we now call "arrangement." Like drivers in a new town, if those listening to a speech aren't provided with aural guideposts, they will likely get lost and feel like they're traveling in and through a foreign town.

This point wasn't lost on ancient orators although some of them including Aristotle, Cicero, and Quintilian, didn't invest as much effort into talking about it as they did other canonical elements. Even so, that's what this lesson is about. In its most basic form, there were four standard parts of arrangement: introduction, facts, proofs, and conclusion. In between the introduction and the conclusion, depending on what type of speech one might give (i.e. deliberative, forensic, or epideictic; see later chapters on the 3 Species of Rhetoric), there was room for additional elements (e.g. narratio, refutatio, etc.).

Thinking solely of the four foundational elements, it is not difficult to understand how a speech without them might seem, well, not very much like a speech. For instance, if a speaker stood up to talk to a group of baseball players and started spouting off about marine biology because that's what was on his mind or was of interest to him, people would be lost. If, however, he gave a few prefatory remarks about his background as a marine biologist and pinpointed a number of transferrable skills from his line of work that might benefit these athletes, it would make more sense.

And imagine, too, if a speaker, just standing up and talking, ended abruptly with no signal that he was about to do so. It would leave everyone confused. Why did he end there? Did something happen or go wrong? Did he forget what he was going to say? Why such a random ending? The introduction and conclusion help provide brackets, if you will, that help hold the framework of the speech together.

In between these brackets, one will find facts and proofs, the latter being those items that substantiate the former. Sticking with the previous example, let's imagine that the marine biologist stated that out of the nearly 32,000 species of fish that have been identified, there's one, the fastest fish known to humans, that could give some pitchers a run for their money: the sailfish. That's a fact.

If the speaker wanted to help substantiate the fact, he could cite proofs. For instance, he could cite the article on "Sailfish" in the *International Wildlife Encyclopedia* that appeals to tests showing that a sailfish traveled 100 yards in 3 seconds, which translates to 68.97 mph. This is simply one of many proofs that the speaker could appeal to. Thus, this proof is backing up the claim, thereby moving its status from claim and codifying it as fact.

Later in this book, after dealing with the 3 species of rhetoric, we'll have the opportunity to refer to what are often perceived to be the 6 most common parts of a speech (exordium, narratio, partitio, confirmatio, refutatio, and peroratio). Now, however, it's time for an activity dealing with the content of this lesson. In the space below, in an effort to connect this lesson with the previous one, write at least three ways you think invention and arrangement work together.

Activity 1: List 3 ways invention & arrangement work together

1.

2.

3.

(3.3) Style

In churches across the globe, preachers and priests don different speaking styles. Some stand behind the pulpit calmly and drone on in a manner worthy of World's Most Monotone Speaker. Others shun the pulpit and pace across the stage yelling and ranting, wearying listeners within the five minutes. Others stand on a platform, wear a big grin, sport a fancy suit, slick back their hair, and act as if they're the congregation's personal wealth coach.

"You idiots! Stop being stupid. Stop being ignorant. You're rejecting God's love. That's what it's about you morons: God's love. Repent, fools!"

Some speaking styles fit individuals better than others. Some styles fit different contexts better than others. And some fit different content better than others. Some styles just don't work or even mix well at all. In the ancient world, there was much talk about style. In fact, the number of words used to describe the manner in which orators spoke is quite large. Most important for this lesson, though, are the 5 virtues and 3 levels of style. Let's look first at the latter.

The 3 levels of style, known as the grand, middle, and plain, each had a different aim. Thus, if speakers knew how they wanted to affect the audience, they could adopt the styles as needed. Indeed, they could mix and match styles—an earmark of a good orator. The grand style had as its chief aim the goal of moving the audience via the use of highly emotive language. The middle sought to please the audience, perhaps via hints of eloquence, and the plain to teach them, often via pointed examples.

Thus, if one were speaking on the subject of racism, here are three statements, one at each level (at least in my opinion), on that topic:

- **Grand**: "It was awful to be Negro and have no control over my life. It was brutal to be young and already trained to sit quietly and listen to charges brought against my color with no chance of defense. We should all be dead. I thought I should like to see us all dead, one on top of the other. A pyramid of flesh with the white folks on the bottom, as the broad base, then the Indians with their silly tomahawks and teepees and wigwams and treaties, the Negroes with their mops and recipes and cotton sacks and spirituals sticking out of their mouths. The Dutch children should all stumble in their wooden shoes and break their necks. The French should choke to death on the Louisiana Purchase while silkworms ate all the Chinese with their stupid pigtails. As a species, we were an abomination. All of us." (Maya Angelou)
- **Middle**: "Racism is man's gravest threat to man - the maximum of hatred for a minimum of reason." (Abraham J. Heschel)
- **Plain**: "Again we have deluded ourselves into believing the myth that Capitalism grew and prospered out of the Protestant ethic of hard work and sacrifice. The fact is that capitalism was built on the exploitation and suffering of black slaves and continues to thrive on the exploitation of the poor – both black and white, both here and abroad." (Martin Luther King, Jr).

Those are the 3 levels of style. And there are, as stated above, 5 virtues of style: purity of speech (i.e. correctness), clarity, vividness (also known as evidence), decorum (i.e. propriety), and eloquence (i.e. ornateness). A brief consideration of each of these, in turn, will prove beneficial. The first, purity of speech, has to do with remaining within the confines of a language's grammatical and syntactic system and playing by its rules. For instance, if you're a Greek speaker, 1) speak Greek correctly, and 2) speak Greek only.

If a speaker deviated from purity standards, it had to be on purpose. Otherwise, he or she would be accused of succumbing to grammatical vices like barbarism (mispronouncing or changing a word) or solecism (butchering a figure of speech or phrase). Doing this on purpose, what we might refer to as a foreignism, is something that most all of us are familiar with. As we have said previously, dropping in a foreign word when speaking in a particular context can put one's cultural awareness or smarts on display. For instance, "How are you, *amigo?*" Or "The *de facto* leader is the President." Deviating from purity for these types of reasons was acceptable and not at all uncommon.

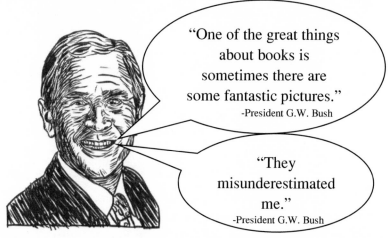

"One of the great things about books is sometimes there are some fantastic pictures."
-President G.W. Bush

"They misunderestimated me."
-President G.W. Bush

The second of the 5 virtues is clarity. This has to do with being well-spoken or articulate. Someone who is articulate has no ambiguity in their speech and, as such, causes no stress or confusion for the listener. Former late show talk host, David Letterman, had a long-running segment on his show while U.S. President, George W. Bush, was in office. It consistently showed Bush violating the clarity principle. Here are a few examples (the quotes above are just for fun):

1) "Tribal sovereignty means that—it's sovereign. I mean, you're a, you've been given sovereignty, and you're viewed as a sovereign entity. And therefore the relationship between the federal government and tribes is one between sovereign entities."

2) "There's an old saying in Tennessee, I know it's in Texas, probably in Tennessee, that says, 'fool me once, shame on, shame on you. Fool me, you can't get fooled again.'"

3) "I know what I believe. I will continue to articulate what I believe and what I believe, I believe what I believe is right."

As you can see, each of these examples is simply hard to follow. There is unnecessary repetition and flawed grammar, among other things, which make them challenging to understand. The next virtue of style is vividness, which was also known as *evidentia*. Even though this looks like the word "evidence," it should not be confused with the English meaning of that term. Rather, if you think of evidence as that which one sees, that's closer to the meaning—it's what is brought before someone's eyes or their mind's eye. It's helping them "see" something through a vivid description or depiction.

The famed poet, Emily Dickinson, excelled at *evidentia*. She was incredibly gifted at bringing things, even abstract things, before the mind's eye. For instance, in a poem titled *Hope is the Thing with Feathers*, she penned these lines:

> *Hope is the thing with feathers, that perches in the soul*
> *And sings the tune without the words, and never stops at all.*
> *And sweetest in the gale is heard, and sore must be the storm*
> *That could abash the little bird that kept so many warm.*
> *I've heard it in the chillest land and on the strangest sea,*
> *Yet never, in extremity, it asked a crumb of me.*

The way Dickinson manages to personify hope and make it something one can visualize is truly impressive. The last lines, which depict hope as speaking but never, not once, asking for anything, is lucid and vivid. And while this is the case, some might contend that her stuff is difficult to understand and, for that reason, may not receive as much praise when it comes to clarity. Agree or disagree? Share your thoughts below.

Activity 1: Does Dickinson pass the purity & clarity tests? Why?

The fourth virtue of style is decorum or propriety. This is the principle that one's speech should fit the context or occasion. In other words, one would not have the chef, Rachel Ray, stand up during a funeral and talk to those in attendance about how to make Meatloaf Brasciole. The words would not fit the occasion and, thus, she would be violating the principle of decorum.

The fifth virtue of style is eloquence or ornateness. Eloquence is concerned with the beauty or aesthetic value of what's said. Things like euphony (pleasing sound), rhythm, cadence, and word choice affect how a listener judges a speaker's eloquence. One can, of course, go overboard with this. If someone tries to use too many rhymes or too many big words, the audience will grow weary and eventually stop listening.

After reading the short paragraph below, excerpted from the book *Davita's Harp*, written by Chaim Potok, discuss whether the 5 virtues of style are present or not.

Very early I became a wanderer. I would walk the streets of each new neighborhood like some hungrily curious fledgling. My parents were frightened at first, for I seemed to slip away in the blink of an eye, and vanish. They scolded me angrily and repeatedly, but it did little good. I needed the streets as antidote to the pernicious confines of the apartments in which we lived. I possessed an uncanny sense of timing and direction and seemed always able to return before serious parental panic set in. In the end my parents grew accustomed to my goings and comings, and left me alone.

Activity 2: Does the excerpt above have the 5 virtues of style?

(3.4) Memory

When it comes to ancient rhetoric and "memory," there's much more to be talked about than simply memorizing things. Indeed, memory was viewed as something of an art form. Many today, as well as many in antiquity, attribute the fourth canon (i.e. memory) to Simonides of Ceos (ca. 556-468 BCE; see Cicero, *On Oratory* 2.353-4 and Quintilian, *Institutes of Oratory* 11.2.11-17).

The story goes that, Simonides, while attending a feast or banquet, got up from his seat to step outside and speak with a messenger. While the two were talking, the building collapsed and killed many. Naturally, he was asked who was inside and, without any trouble, was able to tell the names of everyone.

How? He used the "memory palace" technique. That is, he first envisioned the layout of the room. Then he recalled the seating arrangement. Following that, he was able to stick a face, and thus a name, with each seat. Upon doing this, the realization came that he was able to do it with minimal to no effort at all; it came naturally.

In time, this notion was refined and used by many orators to help recall the structure of their speeches. Quintilian describes this phenomenon in his *Institutes* (11.2.18-21), which I only cite in part here. He says:

Places are picked that are most spacious, marked by much variety, a vast large house also separated into many rooms. In the same (place), that which is notable is diligently fixed to the mind in order that, without delay and hindrance, the parts of it in every thought may be able to be run through...Then, these things they distribute. The first thought they assign to the entrance; the second, think, to the atrium; then, they encircle the rain pool...This being done, soon after it is a memory returned to. Begin from the entry place to review this... (translation mine).

The idea, then, is to pick a place one is very familiar with. Then, zero in on the details of that place and attach a word or image to those details. Recently, I used this approach with one of my children who was trying to memorize the feminine endings for Latin nouns. He had a test on them that day, so, on the way to school, I used the dashboard of the car as well as the visors and mirrors to help him.

For example, we associated the Nominative Singular ending (-a), with the little air vent on the driver's side. Then we stuck the Genitive Singular (-ae) with the air vent near to the passenger's side. Below both vents sat the radio, which we pinned the Dative Singular (-ae) to. Just below that was an opening to put say, a wallet, phone, or some other object into. We associated the Accusative Singular ending (-am) with it. And finally, at the bottom, there was an empty ash tray. We pinned the Ablative Singular (-a) to it.

After we did that, we looked at the dashboard for a few moments intently, striving to take a good mental picture to store in our mind. Once we were ready, we went back through the noun endings several times. Each time we moved from one to the next, I would touch or point out the part of the dashboard we associated with the ending. Within five minutes we had it mastered. We could even look away from the dashboard, which was the idea, and while envisioning it in our minds we were able to recall the connected endings. We did the same sort of thing, as I said, with the visors and mirrors at the front of the car, in order to be able to bring back to mind the plural forms.

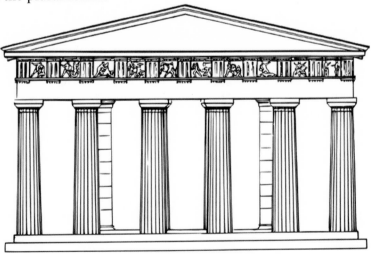

The memory palace technique worked! If you ever travel to an ancient Greek or Roman site, you'll see images above columns and on the frescos. Many times there was a certain scene or pair of scenes depicted above each column. While it was certainly beautiful to look at, this was also a way to aid viewers in remembering each scene and the story it told. Column one had a specific story or set of stories associated with it as did columns two and three and so on. (You can see an example of this in the image on the previous page.)

Like Simonides, my children and I had to exert very little effort to succeed in memorizing the Latin endings. Rather than spend lots of time and energy on rotely memorizing endings and repeatedly getting frustrated, perhaps even finally giving up and admitting defeat, we stored up our information in a vivid and easy-to-retrieve way. That same method can be used in speech giving. For example, lets' say that we're going to give a very short speech on a day at the beach, consisting of about five paragraphs of content.

In paragraph one, I want to talk about the location of the beach. Its name is Electric Beach. Why? Because there is a big power plant across the street. And there are two big pipes that shoot out warm water into the ocean, giving a nice sensation to those who are swimming. In forming a picture of the power plant and the pipes running into the beautiful blue ocean, so I don't forget it, I associate some sort of crazy image—something that'll be stuck forever. Since it's Electric Beach, I imagine those two pipes shooting out bolts of electric and zapping everything in the water. That's paragraph one. Latch on to those pipes shooting out bolts and use that as both a memory point and a talking point.

In the second paragraph, I want to talk about the two pods of dolphins we saw out in the distance. They were beautiful, swimming and jumping, and all with no rush. There were others swimming right along with them, too—an amazing experience. Since I want this to be my talking point, again, I'm going to think of a crazy visual to associate with it. I'll think now of a superhero riding one of the dolphins who is able to deflect electric bolts. He's wearing all purple except for a red mask.

You should have, then, two very potent images in your mind that allow you to remember both of your talking points: 1) pipes from an electric company shooting out electric bolts and zapping everything in the water, and 2) a superhero in a purple outfit and red mask riding a dolphin who is able to defend against electric bolts. In the box below, come up with three very visually strong images to associate with the three remaining talking points you would use to finish the speech.

Activity 1: 3 Vivid images to help recall the talking points
3.
4.
5.

Here, I would like to reiterate one of the main points not just of this chapter but of "memory" as one of the four canons: memory is about the retrieval of images from a storehouse within the mind. It is, therefore, linked to invention. Across the centuries, many great speakers and authors have realized this technique and used it to its fullest. You can and should, too! In fact, as a last effort, try your hand at it. Try, at least once, to tell the story above without consulting any of your notes. That is, do it all by visualizing things in the mind. Have fun!

(3.5) Delivery

One of the things on my "bucket list" is to do a stand-up comedy routine. I've done all sorts of public speaking in other genres and formats. I've delivered sermons, a TED Talk, classroom lectures, thesis defenses, speeches in speech competitions, and I've even sung and done spoken word bits. Never, however, have I done stand-up comedy. It is one of the few types of public speaking left for me to try.

I suppose that one of the reasons I am so interested in stand-up is because it is a different mode of delivery altogether. If one has a decent sense of humor, it is, I think, quite easy to be funny in conversation. If one is an expert in a specific field of study, it isn't the most challenging thing to stand before an audience and, in prose style, speak on that matter. But the job of comics, many of whom are actually the last great truth-tellers in a time when freedom of speech is constantly under fire, seems incredibly challenging.

Even the ancient orator, Quintilian, wrote about the comedians of his day in his *Institutes* and their techniques. At one point, philosophizing on jokes and humor, though, he commented: "While it may appear a light thing, which clowns, mimes, and fools are, indeed, always moved by; nevertheless, it has a force, whether I know it's might or not, which is unable to even be resisted" (6.3.8; *translation mine*). At this point, I want you to write your favorite *clean* joke in the box below and then try to explain in, 1 or 2 sentences, "why" it is funny.

Activity 1: Share a joke and explain "Why" it's funny

50

When Quintilian wrote about delivery, he asserted that it depended chiefly upon two items, namely, voice and gesture (3.3.3). This is no less true of humor than any other type of public speaking. Concerning voice, aspects such as tone, volume, rhythm, cadence, clarity, etc., are all of importance. How a person sounds when speaking is of great importance. Likewise, what one does with their eyes, hands, and body is significant. A raise of the eyebrows, a quick gesture with the hand, or a rapid turn with the body aids in sending the appropriate message. For a comedian, for instance, messing up on one of these can take a funny joke and ruin it.

In fact, as one who has worked with many students preparing to give public speeches, a frequent comment I hear is: "I don't know what to do with my hands while I'm talking." This is a very common issue and, as we know from reading Cicero and Quintilian, among others, it has existed for thousands of years. So, if that's you, know you're in good company. Think just as much about your hand motions as you do your voice, word choice, content, and appearance.

The reality then, just as with now, is that your delivery can help make or break your talk. But then, there was likely much more emphasis on this. Why? In addition to the fact that ancient cultures were oral-aural cultures, there was a lot of focus on the notion that delivering a talk was a form of acting. There was still a difference between acting in a fake context, as in a play, and acting as a public speaker in real life. Yet, in both, logos, pathos, and ethos were always at work. Thinking on these matters, in the box below, describe a time when either you or someone you were watching, bombed the delivery of a speech. What happened? Were any aspects of voice and/or gesture violated?

Activity 2: The Bomb: Who? Why? And How?

(4.1) Deliberative Rhetoric

Did you know that you could be charged with a Class B felony in the state of Alabama if you purchase or own a bear and train it to wrestle humans? Or did you know that, in Arizona, if you try to feed a pig garbage and don't have a permit to do so, you can face legal consequences? Were you aware that, in California, it is evidently illegal to eat a frog that died during a frog jumping contest?[8] Some interesting laws, eh?

"What has two opposable thumbs and is about to make your life un*bear*able? Sincere question, I'd like to know."

Have you ever thought about why each state in the U.S. has laws? Or why your academic institution has rules? Or why your parents have guidelines? If you haven't thought about it, let me be the first to tell you that those strictures are in place to encourage you to both take and maintain a specific course of action and discourage you from taking another course of action. These laws and rules are about the present as well as the future and what you should do in both...like never train a bear to wrestle humans in Alabama, now or ever!

The branch of rhetoric that discourages you from training bears to wrestle, err, I mean deals with your present and future behaviors, is called "deliberative rhetoric." It is, of course, an ancient concept. The orators of long ago described this type of rhetoric as that which urges its audience members to *deliberately* take or not

---

[8] These examples were taken from http://www.businessinsider.com/most-ridiculous-law-in-every-state-2014-2. Site accessed 10/5/17.

take an action or certain course of action. For Aristotle, there were two main talking points, contrastive in nature, within a piece of deliberative rhetoric: worthy and advantageous actions or unworthy and disadvantageous actions (*Rhetoric* 1.3.3).

Using this dialectical approach, that is, this contrast-of-opposites approach, one can talk about things like truth-telling versus lying, moderation versus gluttony, pride versus humility, anger versus patience, and hard work versus sloth. To reiterate a point made previously in this book: deep awareness of and familiarity with topics (what the Greeks referred to as *topoi*) such as these, topics often associated with stories, allowed an orator to stand up and, even at a moment's notice, deliver a speech on that matter.

Figures in the Bible, such as Jesus and Paul, were both very familiar with this. Many times during his life and ministry, Jesus had crowds approach him and, seemingly on the spot, he was able to begin telling stories and parables to teach the listeners. His admonitions often challenged listeners to take certain courses of action in both the present and future. Large portions of some of Paul's letters reveal that he did the same thing. Thus, Jesus and Paul were not merely making everything up but, rather, they were drawing on common *topoi* that they and their listeners would likely have had some familiarity with. In the activity below, find one scene from the Gospel of Mark where Jesus might be drawing on a common topic. Likewise, find a place in Paul's letter titled "Ephesians," where he might be doing this. Write down the verse numbers and briefly describe what you found.

Activity 1: Deliberative Rhetoric & *Topoi* in Mark & Ephesians

Mark:

Ephesians:

(4.2) Forensic Rhetoric

A number of years ago, I was the lead pastor at church in a very rural part of Kentucky. The town was so small, in fact, that there were no stop lights and only one stop sign, which was only necessary because of a blind spot when turning. One morning, as I left my home to walk to the church house, I noticed shattered glass all over the steps to one of the backdoors. There were also a couple of bricks sitting on the steps.

I was a bit nervous but since the place looked empty and it was now day time, I decided to enter. As I went around the building and checked on things, I noticed almost immediately that the church's computer was missing. Once I realized this, I decided to call the police and file a report.

JesusBricks: For when the church locks its doors.

Sadly, even as a small town police outfit with little to do, they weren't very interested in helping me try to figure out who did this. So, I decided to play detective on my own. As I sat in the church house looking around, I noticed that numerous other valuables were still in place. Thus, I grew curious as to why that was the case. Why didn't the thief take those items? I quickly came to the conclusion that whoever broke in must have been familiar with the place, so much so that they knew exactly what they wanted.

They knew the easiest door to break into, they didn't touch any of the other valuables (like a screen or music equipment, etc.), and they knew exactly where the computer was. A suspect came to mind: the new kid in the youth group who we had spent the previous few weeks training to run the computer and sound booth sometimes during the church service.

I went to him that day to ask if he knew anything about it and, of course, he said he didn't. His mom said she knew nothing either. I wasn't buying it. So, I asked some of the other kids in the group to keep an ear and eye out for the computer at school. I didn't tell them whom I was suspecting but, by the end of that day, one of the youth reported back to me that the new kid had a new computer and was showing it off at school.

Therefore, I called the school police the next morning and reported this to them. They went to his locker, did a search, and they found the computer. By the end of that day I received a call confirming that it was found. My initial hunch had been correct; I knew who it was. I filed charges against the teen, hoping to teach him a valuable lesson in terms of legal consequences for such actions. But we also showed him grace and welcomed him back.

When we went to court, I was asked for a testimony. In addition, the evidence was given and the youth was questioned. At one point, someone asked him (I paraphrase here), "When you broke into the church and stole the computer, you knew you were doing wrong, didn't you?" As you can tell, that's a leading question and it presumes that a) this is the proper context to make an accusation against the boy, and b) the boy will answer in the affirmative, admitting his guilt.

That's a long way to get the point but it's worth it because, that single line ending with "...didn't you?" is an example of forensic rhetoric. I should point out here that forensic rhetoric is often called judicial rhetoric, too. This is because in a courtroom, accusations are advanced and proofs offered (from both sides) in an effort to reveal the truth of past actions. It is important to bear in mind, however, that forensic/judicial rhetoric was also used outside of the courtroom with these same intentions.

In John 10:22-30, the religious officials question Jesus about his identity as the Messiah and he offers a defense (known as an *apologia*, from whence we get the word "apologetics") in an effort to reveal the truth of past actions in the present. They say, "If you are the Messiah, tell us clearly." Jesus answered back saying, "I did tell you, but you do not believe." Jesus goes on to explain this a bit more, thus, defending himself. This is an example of forensic rhetoric at work in a specific context.

Jesus offers another "apology" (or "apologetic") earlier in John's narrative, too. John 5:17-45 begins with "In his defense, Jesus said to them." It is clear that Jesus is, in this situation, attempting to reveal the truth of past actions and claims in the present. This, too, is forensic rhetoric. It is also present in John 18:28-38, when Jesus stands before Pilate. This is a formal trial and it reaches its climax near the end of the episode with the following exchange:

33. "...Are you the King of the Jews?"
34. "Are you saying this on your own initiative or have others said it to you about me?"
35. Pilate answered, "I am not a Jew, am I? Your own people and your chief priests handed you over to me. What have you done?"
36. Jesus replied, "My kingdom is not from this world..."
37. Then Pilate said, "So, you are a king!?"
    Jesus replied, "You say that I am a king. I have been born and come into the world for this reason—to testify to the truth. Everyone who belongs to the truth listens to my voice."
38. Pilate asked, "What is truth?"

In the activity below, once you find a modern example of a person or multiple persons using forensic rhetoric write down a relevant portion of their exchange.

Activity 1: An example of forensic rhetoric

(4.3) Epideictic Rhetoric

Heads up: This is a lesson with no pictures. (And psst…so are the next two.) I know you're used to the images by now but, hey, you're just gonna have to deal with it! Keep reading anyway because, trust me, there's some cool stuff to learn about here. Like about that time in 2013, when the talk show host, Stephen Colbert, opened his show with a funny but touching monologue about his mother who had just passed away. He loved her dearly and was clearly proud of her. While on air, he made the following statement about his mother, which, in fact, is just a portion of the overall bit about her:

She made a very loving home for us. No fight between siblings could end without hugs and kisses; although, hugs never needed a reason in her house. Singing and dancing was encouraged, except at the dinner table. She'd trained to be an actress when she was younger and she would teach us to do stage falls by pretending to faint on the kitchen floor. She was fun!

She knew more than her share of tragedy, losing her brother and her husband and three of her sons. But her love for her family and her faith in God somehow gave her strength, not only to go on, but to love life without bitterness and instill in all of us a gratitude for every day we have together.

This type of talk belongs to the branch of rhetoric known as epideictic rhetoric. "Epideictic" is literally just a transliteration of the Greek word επιδεικτικος (*epideiktikos*; pronounced by the Ancient Greeks as: eh-pee-theek-tee-kohs) and means something like "the pointing-at-kind." That is, it's the kind of rhetoric used to point things out, specifically things about people, people groups, towns, etc. For instance, it was common in such speeches to point out a person's lineage, vocational experience, hometown, education, and deeds or a lack thereof.

Not unsurprisingly, Aristotle, when he talked about epideictic, he did so rather dualistically. He described epideictic as having to do with praise or blame. When someone was praised, they were portrayed as living in concert with virtue. When someone was blamed, they were painted as being an heir of and participant in vice. The former was referred to as an encomium while the latter was referred to as an invective.

Thus, the short bit of Colbert's aforementioned speech leads us to classify it as an encomium. And, truthfully, that's what most funeral and/or memorial speeches are. That actually brings up another point about epideictic rhetoric: it is often, though not always, used in ceremonial contexts or ways. Even though Colbert, for instance, wasn't talking about his mom at a funeral here, he used the ceremonial opening segment of his show to speak about her. Since that is usually a catchy, funny bit, to give a more serious talk about something so personally was truly moving to many.

On the flip side, we have invectives. One of history's most well-known invectives is found in Shakespeare's *King Lear*. It isn't used in a ceremonial context but it is still certainly an invective. It comes amid a short conversation between two characters, Kent, who enters in disguise, and Oswald, the steward. Here's how the exchange goes, with the invective coming at the end.

Oswald: Good dawning to thee, friend. Art thou of this house?
  Kent: Ay.
Oswald: Where may we set our horses?
  Kent: I' the' mire.
Oswald: Prithee, if thou lovest me, tell me.
  Kent: I love thee not.
Oswald: Why, then, I care not for thee.
  Kent: If I had thee in Lipsbury pinfold, I would make thee care for me.
Oswald: Why dost thou use me thus? I know thee not.

Kent: Fellow, I know thee.

Oswald: What dost thou know me for?

Kent: A knave, a rascal, an eater of broken meats; a base, proud, shallow, beggarly, three-suited, hundred-pound, filthy, worsted-stocking knave! A lily-livered, action-taking knave! A whoreson, glass-gazing, super-serviceable finical rogue, one-trunk inheriting slave. One that wouldst be a bawd in way of good service; and art nothing but the composition of a knave, beggar, coward, panderer, and the son and heir of a mongrel [dog]; one whom I well beat into clamorous whining if thou deniest the least syllable of thy addition.

And that, my friend, is what you call an invective. Wow! Poor ol' Oswald didn't see that one coming. When you compare and contrast the comment from Kent with the one made by Colbert, it is easy to see just how different they are. The language differs, the tone differs, and the aims differ. Colbert's is an encomium while Kent's is an invective. Those are pretty cool words aren't they—encomium and invective? I think so!

Alright, now that you have an idea of what each looks like, your activity is to choose one or the other and write about carrots. That's right, you're either going to write a word of praise or blame, something showing the inherent vice or virtue of carrots. Don't just sit there, get started.

Activity 1: An encomium or invective for carrots

(4.4) Review, Pt. 1

In this section, your job is to get some review reps in. That'll be your job in the next section, too. Here and there, then, are forty terms that you have encountered thus far throughout the book. They're arranged alphabetically. Your first means of getting a rep in is to write a 1-sentence definition or description for each term on the following pages. Once you've done that, your second rep comes by flipping to the back of the book (i.e. the Glossary) and writing in the same definition/description there. (I know, what a rip off, right—you bought a book with blank glossary entries!) Anyway, happy writing and reviewing!

1 African-Egyptian Orator:

2 Semitic Orators:

3 Appeals of Rhetoric:

3 Species of Rhetoric:

3 Possible Founders of Rhetoric (According to Greek tradition):

3 Styles of Speaking:

5 Canons of Rhetoric:

5 Virtues of Style:

7 Elements of the Rhetorical Triangle:

Apologia/Apology:

Arrangement:

Audience:

Context:

Deliberative Rhetoric:

Dialectical Approach:

Encomium:

Epideictic Rhetoric:

Ethos:

Exigence/Exigency:

Forensic/Judicial Rhetoric:

Fresco:

Grand Style:

Invective:

Invention:

Logos:

(4.5) Review, Pt. 2

Alright, you know the routine so go ahead and get to defining/describing the terms below. Have fun.

Medium:

Memory Palace:

Memory:

Message:

Middle Style:

Pathos:

Plain Style:

Purpose:

Quotative 'Like':

Rhetoric:

Rhetorical Situation:

Rhetorical Triangle:

Simonides:

Speaker:

Stasis:

Structuralism:

Style:

Topoi:

Visual Rhetoric:

Vividness/*Evidentia*:

(5.1) The Exordium

You idiots! How could you be so foolish? Last time we hung out, I let you in on everything. I told you what was up and, I could see with my own eyes that you got it and believed it. And when I saw the light bulbs go on above your heads, I was stoked. But now I'm hearing that you've seriously screwed up. Rumor is, you've taken all the good teaching and trashed it. Or, better yet, you've pawned it in return for polished dung. How could you be such idiots?

Alright, you're probably wondering what the heck is going on, what the heck the preceding paragraph is all about. I don't blame you. Basically, that's my own rendition or paraphrase of the beginning of the Apostle Paul's letter titled Galatians. In my view, it's one of Paul's most fascinating letters and part of the reason for that is because he doesn't start with his normal procedure. Here, Paul pretty much launches right into a verbal assault.

The problem is that the Jews, who had come to pledge allegiance to Christ under his teaching, had started backpedaling. Why? Because a group of false teachers had come behind Paul, twisted Paul's teachings, and even threatened to persecute those who didn't adopt their views. Thus, largely out of fear of persecution and social ostracism, they bent, they caved in.

Umm, Paul was ticked, especially at those preaching circumcision!

I know, right!? That exordium is one thing but Gal 5:12…yikes!

The opening to Galatians is fascinating, however, not only because it is different than the typical intro but also because it is attention-getting. Anyone who had been taught by Paul would have immediately been struck by the choice of words, the tone, and the quick-footed attack. The part of the speech referred to as the intro or the opening was known in antiquity as the exordium.

In the words of Quintilian, the aim of the exordium was to ready the audience, preparing them in such a way that they would have ears to hear the entire speech. The exordium was the place to grab their attention and hold on to it. He argued, and I strongly agree with him, that in this part of the talk one should not use heady metaphors, big words, or quotes.

Why? Well, because metaphors all break down at some point, so, it's a good way to lose people. Moreover, big words can outright confuse listeners. And a quote is a waste because it's not your words—it's someone else saying what they think about your topic. People are there to listen to you and what you think; they're not there to listen to others. Trust me when I tell you to trust this time-tested wisdom.

Another piece of advice I would give is to ignore the books that tell you to write your introduction last. Some suggest that you should write it after everything else is done. I disagree. I find that writing the exordium first and leaving it open for modification is the most helpful. That is because it sets the tone and course for what comes next. It allows the first segue to happen naturally rather than forcing it. That, in turn, sets the pattern for everything else that follows. My advice: write the intro first and leave it open for modification during the entirety of the writing process.

As Joseph Colavito notes, in antiquity there were two approaches to writing the exordium: 1) the direct approach, known as *proomion* by the Greeks and the *principium* by the Romans, and 2) the indirect approach, known as the *ephodos* by the Greeks and the *insinuatio* by the Romans.[9] Being aware of one's audience was

---

[9] Joseph Colavito, "Exordium," in *Encyclopedia of Rhetoric and Composition: Communication from Ancient Times to the Information Age,* ed. T. Enos (GRLH 1389; New York: Routledge, 1996), 247-8.

critical in choosing which approach to take. If one chose the direct approach, it signaled that they were on the same page with the audience and, as such, the well-disposed listeners would gladly lend an ear.

If, however, one chose the indirect approach, it signaled their awareness of difference and, perhaps, hostility, between the speaker and audience. One could still build rapport with the audience using this method but they would do so by spelling out where their agreements exist. Only after doing that and likely speaking in large and/or vague generalities, could they begin to address the disagreements between parties. In short, it's like buttering up a parent with compliments before telling them you drove the car through your neighbor's mailbox and fence—something I once did, not joking!

Now that you know what an exordium is, take a moment to look up Gal 1:1-10. Once you do that, your job is to rewrite the introduction in your own words, like I did at the start of this lesson.

Activity 1: Rewrite the exordium of Gal 1:1-10 in your words

(5.2) The Narratio, Propositio, and Partitio

In this lesson, the plan is to talk about the three topics mentioned above in the title. They are ordered this way because, well, that's how they were often arranged in the ancient world. Now, I don't know if one could make a case that guys like Aristotle, Cicero, and Quintilian, guys who really liked categorizing, labeling, and arranging things, had OCD or not, but if such a fact ever came to light none of us should be all that surprised.

I DON'T ALWAYS INVITE FRIENDS OVER

BUT WHEN I DO, I MAKE SURE THEY HAVE OCD SO MY PLACE GETS CLEANED

In all seriousness (I know, how can I even say that with the picture to the left!), we should be thankful that these guys were so attentive to detail. Despite the fact that Quintilian's 12 volumes on rhetoric were lost for thousands of years and accidentally found in a monastery basement, as you have already recognized in the book you're currently reading, his influence is very important. Unlike Aristotle, who balked a bit at the notion of narratio, Qunitilian believed it was necessary when speaking. In his view, the narratio was what helped set the stage for the remain- of the talk. This was the place, then, to do the following: a) state the main point, b) clarify terms, and c) offer a brief and relevant bit of backstory pertinent to both the present and future, perhaps using history or fact.

A recent example of this can be found in a former President, Barack Obama's, speech at the 2012 Democratic National Convention. In his nomination acceptance speech he said the following (I put what I believe to be the heart of the narratio in bold):

"*I know that campaigns can seem small and even silly. Trivial things become big distractions. Serious issues become sound bites and the truth gets buried under an avalanche of money and advertising. If you're sick of hearing me approve this message, believe me, so am I.*

But when all is said and done, when you pick up that ballot to vote, you will face the clearest choice of any time in a generation. *Over the next few years, big decisions will be made in Washington, on jobs and the economy; taxes and deficits; energy and education; war and peace—decisions that will have a huge impact on our lives and our children's lives for decades to come.*

On every issue, the choice you face won't be just between two candidates or two parties. It will be a choice between two different paths for America. A choice between two fundamentally different visions for the future. Ours is a fight to restore the values that built the largest middle class and the strongest economy the world has ever known; the values my grandfather defended as a soldier in Patton's Army; the values that drove my grandmother to work on a bomber assembly line while he was gone."

DOC, I've read through this OCD checklist 111 times and, honestly, I'm still not sure if I have it.

I identify the boldened sentence as the heart of the narratio because it is what sets the score for all that is to come. He has set the backstory in the preceding sentences and will, in fact, continue to do so after this statement. But his main point concerns choices, something he states in this sentence. He will repeat that word numerous times afterward, too. And he goes on to clarify what he means by 'choice' and the implications of choosing, cloaking it in the garb of the good choices he believes his family members made. All of this is done with an eye to both the present and future.

Following the narratio is the propositio. Now, this is another element that was up for debate among the ancient orators. But rather than rehearsing that here, I simply want to draw attention to what it is: either a) a snapshot of what's to come, or b) the specific accusations/charges being leveled against someone or something. In modern parlance, a common quip among those educating speakers is "tell the audience what you're going to tell them, tell them, then tell them what you told them." I certainly heard that in speaking classes I took. For what it's worth, I don't think it's a bad idea.

Men, that's why the 1st rule of our OCD club is that we must establish a 2nd rule—to have an even number of rules.

What might be a bad idea is to give too much detail up front, to be condescending when giving the detail, or to simply presume that all your listeners already know all the details you do. In all truthfulness, you can do this in ways that do not make you seem like Mr. or Mrs. Obvious. If you want to be one of those characters, that's up to you and, perhaps, can work well depending on your audience. For instance, if you're speaking to a group of youngsters, spelling it out three times (or more) may be a good idea. It may help it "stick."

As far as the charges or accusations go, you can probably already figure that forensic rhetoric is in view here. Or maybe an invective. Either way, this is where you're going to do the court room move—turn to the jury and say something like, "And jury, this is why—his negligence, his repeated history of abuse, his proneness to company cover-up—I believe Mr. Weinstein should be found guilty, a truth I will further substantiate in due time." When you say something like that, everyone knows the point and everyone knows, in general, what you're going to talk about in the future.

Closely related to the propositio is the partitio (also known as the divisio). Have a little fun and read that last sentence three times in a row very quickly. (Truth time: I tried it and failed on my first attempt.) The partitio is the portion of the speech that outlines, whether generically or specifically, what is to come. Sound familiar? Yeah, it should. Because it is quite like the propositio. Perhaps the main difference would be that in the propositio one is outlining all the "main" points or arguments of the speech.

♫ IF YOU'RE OCD AND YOU KNOW IT WASH YOUR HANDS ♫

Presumably, after one signals the main points of the speech, when they proceed to giving the rest of it, they will identify when each argument comes up. Sometimes the shifts between points can be subtle. This, however, is not recommended by the ancient orators; the switches should be noted and easily identified by listeners.

One way to think of it is to imagine a book. You can view the Table of Contents as the place where the main arguments are first spelled out and then the chapter headings and/or subheadings, which should be the same as the Table of Contents, as the places where these matters are revisited and addressed at more length. Of course, in ancient Greek and Latin texts, chapter headings and subheadings were rarer so things like key words, spacing in a physical manuscript, or other such things could function as helpful identifiers. Okay, well, that's it for now. You've read a lot, so, no activity for this chapter. Oh, and please don't be offended at the OCD jokes, once I got started, I couldn't stop thinking about it. ☺

(5.3) Confirmatio

As with the Encomium, Invective, and Refutatio (see the next lesson), later in this book you will revisit the current focus: Confirmatio. In a nutshell, the confirmatio is meant to prove the propositio and/or partitio via proofs and facts. For Aristotle, the narratio and the refutatio were the two most important aspects of any speech; without them, it just wouldn't work. This is why it was emphasized early on as part of the progymnasmata—the ancient curriculum used to teach literary, speech, and rhetorical principles. (The progymnasmata is also the focus of the second half of this book! Thus, you'll become very familiar with it in due course.)

At this point, recall that a propositio is either a) a snapshot of what's to come, or b) the specific accusations/charges being leveled against someone or something. Thus, the confirmatio is going to bring out proofs to substantiate the previously offered snapshot or accusations/charges. In thinking about this, I, as a former minister, recalled the general wedding manual.

Already Emotional, She Bolted When She Saw The Cake In Tiers

A minister's wedding manual walks step-by-step and word-by-word through a wedding ceremony. Traditionally, the first thing to do, after the initial seating and music, is to approach the front of the crowd and offer a prayer. Once the prayer concludes, the minister will speak for the first time saying something like, "We are gathered together today as witnesses in the sight of God in order to join together this man and this woman in holy matrimony." This is the propositio.

Much of what the minister says following this will be in the form of a confirmatio. (Often, in a wedding ceremony a partitio isn't needed because there's a detailed schedule in the bulletin.) In other words, the minister will go on to prove or confirm his or her statement. He or she may describe what it means to be "gathered together," to be "witnesses in the sight of God," and what the purpose of joining a man and woman together in "holy matrimony" means.

For instance, part of the gathering together includes members of the wedding party giving a son or daughter in marriage. Sometimes, too, a minister will say something to the effect of, "If there is anyone here who finds reason why these two shall not be wed, speak now or forever hold your peace." This is a directive issued to those in attendance—a call for them to speak if they so desire. It is an acknowledgement of the gathering together as witnesses.

Concerning "holy matrimony," things like prayer, communion, candle lighting, vows, the explanation of a ring's significance, a sermon, etc., all give meaning to these terms. These are speech-acts that confirm that holy matrimony is being enacted right in the presence of everyone.

Maybe another way to conceive of this is simply in terms of a research paper. Here, students have a thesis, gather data to support the thesis, and then marshal that data to finally confirm or prove the thesis. That, too, is a confirmatio. Ha, maybe I should have just said that at the beginning and saved you all this reading! Oh well, you'll get over it. For now, take consolation in the fact that you escape an activity on confirmatio since you'll have one at a later point in the book. Thank me later!

(5.4) Refutatio

Just by looking at the title of this lesson, your English sensibilities likely give you some idea of what it's about. If you thought "refereeing" or "refuturing" (that's not even a thing—redoing the future!) then I'm sorry to be the bearer of bad news, but your English sensibilities are off. Like, way off. If, however, you thought of "refute," as in, to refute someone's claims, then I'm less worried about you. Don't get me wrong, I still have my worries about some of you—you know who you are!

In ancient rhetoric, the point in a speech when you refute someone's claims is known as the refutatio. What a coincidence, eh?! To refute an argument means to go against it in an attempt to disprove it. So, in the refutatio, just as in the confirmatio, some proofs are going to be needed.

Imagine, for instance, that a rumor has been started and is spreading around school about you. (Hey, don't look at me, seriously, I would, uh…., never do such a thing!) One of the things you're likely going to try to do, if it's not something that truly happened, is start mounting a defense (apologia) to undermine those making the false claims. When you do that, your aim is to refute them.

73

In a speech, especially a political speech or any talk that falls within the genre of judicial rhetoric, the refutatio is immensely important. Yet, in academic circles, too, where new research is presented, part of the protocol in presenting one's own data is to have assessed others' data showing how it is problematic or unreliable or wrong. That portion of your research paper or talk is the refutatio.

This, too, is where you may have the chance to refute any questions you believe might be leveled against your claims. In other words, if your findings are novel and no one has yet heard them, then no one will have had the chance to try to debunk them. Yet, as soon as they see or hear your research, they will likely try to do that. Why? Because that's how academics roll! Scholars love arguing with one another. As a scholar I say that a bit in jest but also realizing that we don't just argue for the fun of it, at least most of us anyway, but we argue because we all have a shared goal of making solid strides in our fields of study. Thus, shoddy research and weak claims just don't cut it.

But, as the presenter of this new research, you can anticipate how your opponents might challenge and/or interrogate you. This, too, is part of the refutatio. Guys like Aristotle, Cicero, and Quintilian took the refutatio very serious. They talked about things like using comparisons and contrasts effectively in the refutatio, as well as syllogisms and enthymemes. And I suppose that since I have brought those up, this would be a great place to explain what they are.

To start, then, let's understand the term 'syllogism' as a conclusion. Or, to be just a tad more specific, a conclusion one has reached by way of a few logical steps. Stated more simply, this all has to do with the thought you put into reaching a conclusion. Admittedly, sometimes we put a lot of thought into things but, at other times, we fail pretty miserably. Here's an example of a well-structured syllogism:

(Major) Premise 1: All burritos from that restaurant taste good.
(Minor) Premise 2: These burritos are from that restaurant.
Conclusion: Therefore, these burritos taste good.

What is going on here is that the first premise, which is also known as the major premise, offers a general claim from someone who believes it to be true. Next, the minor or second premise is offered, which, as you can see, is a bit more narrow and specific. Finally, if the logic is sound, the conclusion reached will prove true or accurate. So, the syllogism is, to repeat what was stated above, the conclusion and the thought put into reaching it. Here's a not-so-good example:

(Major) Premise 1: All pirates from Neverland have cool accents.
(Minor) Premise 2: These pirates are from Neverland.
Conclusion: Therefore, these pirates like burritos.

As you can see, there is a breakdown in logic here and, as a result, a breakdown in the conclusion. Hopefully, that doesn't take too much explaining—it's pretty straightforward. Within the discussion about syllogisms in antiquity, the philosopheme, epicheireme, and enthymeme were spoken of.

A philosopheme is, as the name suggests, related to philosophy, particularly in having a philosophical motif. It is also known by the name "demonstrative syllogism." For Aristotle, at least, this had to do with showing or demonstrating knowledge advanced and expressed in the conclusion that was already presumed or known to be true. This may be done in the service of rhetoric—the art of persuasion—but is also different than it. Why? Because persuasion produces opinion while demonstration exposes knowledge:

(Major) Premise 1: All humans must breathe air to survive.
(Minor) Premise 2: I am a human.
Conclusion: Therefore, I breathe air to survive.

Here, the syllogism moves beyond simple rhetoric—it doesn't aim to persuade; rather, it aims to demonstrate that which is already known. In the activity below, construct a syllogism based on 1 John 5:1 using the formula given above.

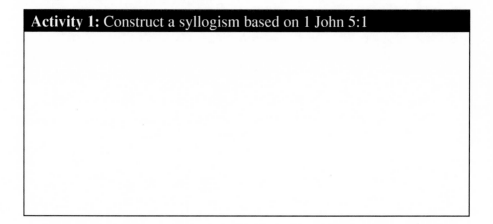

Activity 1: Construct a syllogism based on 1 John 5:1

Another type of syllogism was the epicheireme (or: epichireme). For Aristotle, the epicheireme was more complex than the standard syllogism in that it offered proofs after each premise. It takes the form that is provided in my modified example from Cicero.

(Major) Premise 1: Orderly things are better than non-orderly ones.
(Major) Proof 1: A sailor's orderly itinerary prevents getting lost.
(Minor) Premise 2: An orderly universe is better than all
                alternatives.
(Minor) Proof 2: The order of night and day keeps humans safe.
Conclusion: Therefore, the universe is orderly.

Now, take a moment and complete the activity on the following page. Give an answer as to why one might use a philosopheme or epicheireme in a refutatio.

Activity 2: Why use the philosopheme or epicheireme in a refutatio?

Finally, the last type of syllogism to consider is the enthymeme. Simply put, an enthymeme is a syllogism in which one of the premises is missing. Here is an example:

(Major) Premise 1: His family has served this town for decades.
Conclusion: Therefore, he cannot be guilty of this crime.

What is the hidden or missing premise here?

(Minor) Premise 2: People who serve in this town for decades cannot be guilty of committing crimes.

Alright, rather than make you do another activity, your job is to complete the following both here and in the glossary.

Enthymeme:

Epicheireme:

Philosopheme:

Refutatio:

Syllogism:

(5.5) Peroratio

The way you end a speech matters. It matters a lot. The ancient Roman orators referred to this part of the speech as the peroratio. This comes from the Latin preposition, per, which means "through" or "across," and the noun, "oratio," which means "speech." If you put the two together, you get: "through/across the speech." Similarly, if we break down the word "conclusion," we realize that it comes from the preposition "com" (often changes to "con") meaning "with" and "claudo," meaning "to close." Thus, the conclusion is what you "close with."

In joining these two concepts, we realize that what you close with should be the things you talked about through the speech. It goes back to the maxim I mentioned in an earlier lesson: tell the audience what you're going to tell them, tell them, then tell them what you told them. In short: summarize. The act of summarizing was, in fact, one of several things Cicero believed a rhetor should do in the peroratio.

So, if you had 4 main points throughout the body of your speech, at this point you want to go back through and summarize them. At the same time, you should strive to bring the audience into agreement with your conclusions about these matters. According to Cicero, one strategy is, in the peroratio, to appeal to ethos. In doing so, you can either a) tell a moving story that will cause the audience to sympathize and/or empathize with you, or b) say something about opponents that will leave your listeners in a state of questioning or not trusting them.

For Cicero, and Quintilian, too, the peroratio should be brief. This is not a place to drone on. Moreover, it is your last chance to build rapport with the audience, so, leave them with something to think on and leave them in a state where their disposition toward you and your ideas is favorable. This is precisely why I am adamant about never ending a speech, sermon, chapter, etc., with a quote from someone else—as many are fond of doing. You don't want someone to think about the words of another person; rather, you want them thinking about what you had to say. Therefore, as with the introduction, make the final statement yours. And make sure you nail it!

Now, at the advice of Cicero and Quintilian, I'm going to consider this the peroratio of the first half of this book. In the course of the last twenty-five lessons, you have spent time learning about the foundations of rhetoric. You have learned about the history of rhetoric, what rhetoric is, the 5 canons of rhetoric, stasis theory, the rhetorical triangle, the three species of rhetoric, and more. A lot of ground has been covered. You have done well to get to this point and are to be commended. Well done!

In the second portion of this book, starting with Lesson 6.1, you will learn about the rhetorical exercises that ancient teachers of rhetoric used to educate their students. These were called "progymnasmata." I believe you will enjoy it and find it beneficial because it will help broaden your repertoire as a thinker, writer, and speaker. For now, I will simply ask one thing of you, namely, to offer a definition/description of the words peroratio and progymnasmata below and then to take those same epithets and add them to the glossary at the back of the book. Again, kudos for getting to this point!

PS: How did I do in terms of using those last two paragraphs as a peroratio? Look at them again and think about that.

Peroratio:

Progymnasmata:

(6.1) Fable

Chances are, you've never lived on the moon. Likewise, I'm guessing that you didn't just crawl out from under a rock. And, more than likely, you probably haven't been in hiding for an extended measure of time. So, I'm going to assume that you're familiar with the term "fable." I'm going to make the assumption, too, that you've heard a fable before.

If my assumption is correct, then you've probably also heard or been taught or come to the conclusion about what a fable is, how to describe, and/or define it. For example, it is common to describe fables as short fictional accounts that aim to teach moral lessons. The problem with this is that there are some fables, both modern and ancient, that are not short. Moreover, there are some that do not seem to have the intention of teaching moral lessons.

So, what is a fable then? How do we define it? Well, just to get on the same page, let's agree to proceed with the following definition of a fable, one that comes from my translation of Alius Theon, one of the four main authors of progymnasmata in antiquity:

μῦθός ἐστι λόγος ψευδὴς εἰκονίζων ἀλήθειαν.
A fable is a story of falsehood depicting truth.

Note that Theon's use of the word μῦθος (transliterated as "myth") is translated here as "fable."

From my perspective, when Theon uses the word "falsehood" here (the word from which we get "pseudo" in English), what he means is something like "fiction." In other words, he's talking about something that didn't necessarily happen but still conveys a truth and, in fact, may convey that truth in a more profound way than a non-fiction story.

This is why for centuries, despite many of the criticisms leveled at them, Aesop's fables have lived on—they deliver profound truths. During the first several centuries of the Common

Era, numerous Greco-Roman authors, such as Phaedrus, Babrius, and Avianus, were already handling and elaborating on these fables.

Authors of Surviving Progymnasmata

Author / Century CE
+ Alius Theon / 1st
+ Hermogenes / 2nd
+ Aphthonius / 4th
+ Nicolas Myra / 5th

In general, the progymnasmata exercises were meant to a) help students choose the right genre to convey their message and make their point(s), and b) to help students master the principles of rhetoric and then prove that mastery to their teachers. Yet, more specifically, in some of the progymnasmata, teaching students exercises on fables was often the first and least complicated act toward achieving this goal.

For a writer like Hermogenes of Tarsus, having animals think or speak or act, was an earmark of the fable. Moreover, attaching certain stock characteristics to these animals was key. For instance, peacocks were associated with beauty, foxes with wisdom, and monkeys with imitators. The use of thinking and speaking animals to represent specific characteristics was a way to a) leave a fable open-ended with regard to interpretation, and b) create distance between the author/speaker and the audience so that offense isn't directly taken.

Below, I have included an Ethiopian fable. Your task is threefold: 1) read the fable; 2) identify what the characters and/or objects mentioned in the story might represent; and, 3) analyze it with regard to whether it has a moral and, if so, explain what it is.

An Ox and Donkey

One day, an ox went to a nearby donkey on the farm and said, "I'm sick of working. I'm always tired. How can I get some rest?" The donkey replied, "Tomorrow, when the master comes, lie on your back and act like your stomach hurts and you are sick." The next day, the ox did this and, as a result, the master made the donkey carry the plow. At the end of the day, the donkey was exhausted.

Happy about having had the opportunity to rest, the ox approached the donkey and bragged about how good his day was and how good he felt. So, he asked, "Give me another way to trick the master." This time the donkey said, "I heard today that, if you don't work around here, the master will slaughter you." The next day, the ox decided to make himself available for the plow.

- Who are the characters in the story?

- Do the characters, objects, and/or setting seem to represent something?

- Does the story have a moral? If so, what is it?

Finally, just below, define the term and then add your definition to the glossary in the back of the book.

Fable:

(6.2) Fable

Now that you have encountered a fable and, to some degree, analyze it, the next step is to dig back into it. Rather than rush to leave it because you've already read and thought about it, the goal is to spend a bit more time getting to know it even better. Yet, at the same time, you're going to begin modifying it and putting it into your own words.

This begins, for us, the process the ancients referred to as imitatio or mimesis. In this book you will go through two steps in the process of imitatio: 1) rewording and retelling, and 2) borrowing core elements for a new story. The focus of this lesson is on the former and, in the next lesson, the latter comes into view. So, for now, your job is to take the same Ethiopian fable from the previous chapter and to begin rewording it so that, ultimately, you can retell it in your own words and context.

The way to begin is to simply take each sentence, one a time, on its own. Within the sentence, try to discern what you might be able to change, remove, or add to bring your unique flavor to the story. Bear in mind, however, that changing the setting, character, and moral of the story is not the goal here. Your aim is to simply change things to flavor the story in your own way.

In antiquity, strict protocols often existed for retelling a story. But the level of strictness depended on things like how foundational and important the story was to the culture. If, for instance, you were dealing with a key religious story, very little change could often take place. Yet, if you were telling a very common children's story or a stock fable, the protocols were loosened substantially.

What we're aiming for here is fidelity to the original story while also having some flexibility to change it. The Ethiopian fable, then, can be reworded and, as such, retold, but the core and its main elements should not be changed too much. In short: Use your creativity to tell the same story in a fresh yet reliable way; honor tradition while, at the same time, allowing your language and context to bring a new color to things.

Here are a few examples of sentences from the fable and how I might change them.

Original: *One day, an ox went to a nearby donkey on the farm and said, "I'm sick of working. I'm always tired. How can I get some rest?"*

Reworded: *As the afternoon sun finally gave in and began to set on the farm, an exhausted and dragging ox approached his friend, a donkey, and grumbled, "I'm so over all this working and forever being tired! What can an ox do to catch a break 'round here?"*

> **Comments**: As you can see, if you compare the two sentences, they essentially say the same thing. The reworded version, however, reveals my attempts to add a bit more description.

Original: *The donkey replied, "Tomorrow, when the master comes, lie on your back and act like your stomach hurts and you are sick."*

Reworded: Although he seemed to be taking a moment to think, the donkey, just too tired to respond right away, eventually piped up saying, "Look, tomorrow, when the master comes play sick. Lie on your side, groan aloud, cringe, and hold your stomach."

> **Comments**: Once again, all I have really done here is embellish. I haven't changed the meaning of the sentence; I've simply added some details. I did, however, make the decision to change "Lie on your back" to "Lie on your side" because that seems more like what an ox would actually do.

Okay, now it's your turn. Take the fable in its entirety and begin working toward a full rewording and retelling. Remember: the goal is not to change the story in any dramatic way. You're simply spicing it up with your authorial flair. Leave the core elements alone.

Just below I've included the fable, sentence-by-sentence, in its entirety. Write your reworded sentences in the "Reworded" sections, creating a sort of interlinear that allows you to compare and contrast yours with the original. (Note: *If you need more space than what's provided, feel free to use a blank piece of paper and simply stash it between the pages here when you're done.*)

Original: *One day, an ox went to a nearby donkey on the farm and said, "I'm sick of working. I'm always tired. How can I get some rest?"*

Reworded:

Original: *The donkey replied, "Tomorrow, when the master comes, lie on your back and act like your stomach hurts and you are sick."*

Reworded:

Original: *The next day, the ox did this and, as a result, the master made the donkey carry the plow.*

Reworded:

Original: *At the end of the day, the donkey was exhausted.*

Reworded:

Original: *Happy about having had the opportunity to rest, the ox approached the donkey and bragged about how good his day was and how good he felt.*

Reworded:

Original: *So, he asked, "Give me another way to trick the master."*

Reworded:

Original: *This time the donkey said, "I heard today that, if you don't work around here, the master will slaughter you."*

Reworded:

Original: *The next day, the ox decided to make himself available for the plow.*

Reworded:

(6.3) Fable

Hello, sunshine! Welcome to Lesson 6.3. As noted in the previous lesson, the goal here is to continue working on our imitative or mimetic skills. You've had the chance to read, analyze, and retell the Ethiopian fable you first encountered in Lesson 6.1. Now the aim is to extract and borrow the core elements from that to create a new story. It should be noted that this is different from what you will do in Lesson 6.4, that is, create an entirely new fable. There, you will not be asked to borrow from the Ethiopian fable; rather, the intent is to come up with something completely original. More on that when we get there!

The way to get started here is to identify and extract the elements you'll need to borrow. These will likely be setting, characters, and the moral or point of the story. To make it a bit more interesting, you might change the setting or reverse the roles of the characters. Try, however, to keep the moral the same. You want to make the same point using some of the same details but by telling a new story. I'll give an example of how I would do this. Once you finish reading that, you go ahead and give it a shot. (Note: *Sometimes, as with many of Aesop's fables, the last line tells the moral or point of the story if there is one. The Ethiopian fable above did not do that. If, however, you'd like to, you can give it a try. I will do that here.*)

The Ox and Donkey

Within the heart of a certain city there were numerous tiny plots of farmland. Every day, as the sun rose, a farmer loaded large potato sacks on to the backs of his ox and donkey. He walked behind them, cracking a whip, as he drove them to the local market where his wife ran a potato stand. For twelve hours per day, and sometimes fourteen, the ox and donkey hauled potatoes back and forth.

One day, while standing in the market and being unloaded, the ox saw a fruit stand. For the next week, he eyeballed that stand and became obsessed with it. He said to the donkey, "Have you noticed the fruit stand at the market?" The donkey replied, "Of course, how could I miss it?" The donkey replied, "Tomorrow, I want to get a piece of fruit. How can I make that happen?"

The donkey, without hesitation, replied, "After we're unloaded and just as we begin to leave the market passing that stand, I will fall down. When I do, grab your piece of fruit and eat it quickly. When you're finished, I'll stand back up." So, as they began to leave the ox and donkey did just as they had planned. But when the donkey fell, the master began hitting him with the whip. Within seconds, he was bleeding and swelling. The ox, however, was all smiles as he enjoyed his stolen piece of fruit.

Encouraging another to engage in vice will backfire on you.

Okay, now it's your turn. Borrow the moral, among other things, from our Ethiopian fable, and come up with your own. Use the space below to do so. (Note: *If you need more space than what's provided, feel free to use a blank piece of paper and simply stash it between the pages here when you're done.*)

PS: *For fun and, if you have time, create a fable in the tradition of a Madlib (Google that term if you need to!). Ask someone to fill in the blanks and then read their response back to them.*

(6.4) Fable

In this lesson, you have a simple task to carry out: create an original fable. Now that you've read, analyzed, and twice imitated an already existing fable, it is your turn to invent. So, go ahead and look down to the bottom of this page and then at the next, too. See all that white space? That's where you'll put your fable and, who knows, maybe your fable will live on for ages to come. By the way, I would encourage you to try the following approach:

1. Come up with a setting, knowing that this may take some research;
2. Come up with characters, knowing that this, too, may take some thinking about and perhaps research;
3. Decide on a moral/point;
4. Decide on a plot;
5. Begin writing;
6. Go back through and polish up your language.

(6.4) Fable

[Use the extra space below for your composition if needed.]

(6.5) Fable

This is the final lesson working with fables. The aim here is to create a sequel to the fable you composed in Lesson 6.4. So, you should somehow include the same characters. You can change the setting and the moral if you'd like. You might also add characters or, if you're only going to use the same ones, try casting them in the role of someone's or something's memory. For instance, you could tell a story about a snake who remembers either the ox or donkey or both.

Changing the setting could really go a long way, too. Perhaps you could put the ox and mule in a house, a jail, on a ship, in a church building, etc. Once you have your characters and setting selected, it might be easier to choose a moral or point. On the other hand, it could be advantageous to pick a moral or point and allow that to shape who the characters are, where they are, and what they're doing.

Therefore, with your previous fable in mind, once again try to utilize the following steps in your writing process.

1. Come up with a setting, knowing that this may take some research;
2. Come up with characters, knowing that this, too, may take some thinking about and perhaps research;
3. Decide on a moral/point;
4. Decide on a plot;
5. Begin writing;
6. Go back through and polish up your language.

[Use the extra space below for your composition if needed.]

(7.1) Narrative

Socrates once remarked that "The unexamined life is not worth living." If I could riff on his comment in light of the topic of this and the next several lessons, I might say this: "A life without story is a not worth living." Story grounds us in reality and yet allows us to imagine. Story reminds us of who we are, where we came from, and that we're all headed somewhere. Story is life and life is story.

In antiquity, the importance of telling tales, whether long or short, historical or fictional, cannot be underestimated. That is why, after all, storytelling was included in the progymnasmata. There was a great interest in creating narratives, remembering them, and passing them on. In addition, narrative was used as a means of persuasion—it was a rhetorical endeavor.

Ancient religious communities held firmly to their stories, preserving them and passing them on as a means of persuading all adherents and outsiders of who they were and what they were about. In epideictic settings, stories recalling how an individual lived well could be shared. And in forensic settings, vivid narratives could persuade a jury one way or the other.

The Bible, too, is replete with stories. Yet, in a very fascinating way, those stories combine to create one large narrative about God's people. Perhaps even more amazingly, Scripture seems to suggest that those who are part of God's people are also part of the story. Thus, even though the biblical canon is closed, God is still writing his story and is doing so through his faithful children. So, again, I say: story is life and life is story.

In this lesson, we begin thinking about how to tell a story and, even more, how to tell it well. As with the previous lessons on fables, we'll follow the same basic outline here. That means we'll begin by reading a story and analyzing its constituent parts. The story below is a very short one that is biographical in nature. Since I'm from Kentucky, I thought I'd write a brief narrative about one of the state's most famous icons.

[Read the story below and then answer the questions that follow.]

A Colonel of Truth

When you're six-years old and your father dies, what do you do? And when you're ten-years old and you're left to help your mother fend for your younger brother and sister, have you any choice but to do so? And what does it say about you, then, when you're forty-years old and successfully running your own business? What about when you're forty-five-years old and have bestowed upon you your state's highest public honor?

Surprisingly, answers to such questions may be found in the life story of Harland Sanders. Although born in Indiana, he was a Kentucky boy at heart. In time, and as the founder of Kentucky Fried Chicken, he became known the world over as Colonel Sanders, the iconic name that matched its iconic portraiture—black-rimmed frames, white hair, and a black string tie.

Sanders lost his father at a young age and, as he grew, by default, he assumed big responsibilities within his family—including putting food on the table. His early years of work experience served him well and, in his thirties, he was running a restaurant of such renown that it not only became—and remains—a state landmark, but earned him the public rank of Kentucky Colonel. A handful of years later, upon franchising his restaurant, it also earned him hundreds of millions of dollars. And never again was putting food on the table a concern in the Sanders family. When you do those kinds of things, it speaks volumes about you, about your character, and about the unbridled spirit of Kentuckians.

- What is the point of the story?

- Who is the narrator? Is it a first-person or third-person account?

- What is the narrator's point of view?

- Does the introduction grab and hold your attention?

- Does the story share internal or external conflict?

- If there is conflict present is it resolved?

- Is there a climactic point in the story?

As you move forward in your attempts to understand and work on narratives, it would be beneficial to keep these questions in mind. Not only will they aid you in reading other works but they will also help you in composing, whether you're composing something entirely original or not. And that's what you'll begin to do in the following lesson. See you there!

Ps: Define "narrative" here and then add your definition to the glossary in the back of the book.

Narrative:

(7.2) Narrative

This lesson asks you to retell the narrative from the preceding lesson, you know, the one about Colonel Sanders. Unlike our engagement with fables, however, we're going to attempt something just a bit different here. Why? Because Quintilian (*Institutes of Oratory*, 2.4.15) said so! More specifically, his suggestion was to take a story and to tell it in reverse or to start from the middle, presumably placing the introductory material next. Sometimes the goal was to still tell the same story and at other times change it dramatically.

So, that's your task: find a way to retell the Colonel Sanders story using one of these techniques. You can change sentence and paragraph order, use different words and punctuation, and find a way to tell the same short story in a different way. I've included the story again below for reference. Use the blank space on the following pages to compose. Once you've finished, answer the questions. And...go!

A Colonel of Truth

When you're six-years old and your father dies, what do you do? And when you're ten-years old and you're left to help your mother fend for your younger brother and sister, have you any choice but to do so? And what does it say about you, then, when you're forty-years old and successfully running your own business? What about when you're forty-five-years old and have bestowed upon you your state's highest public honor?

Surprisingly, answers to such questions may be found in the life story of Harland Sanders. Although born in Indiana, he was a Kentucky boy at heart. In time, and as the founder of Kentucky Fried Chicken, he became known the world over as Colonel Sanders, the iconic name that matched its iconic portraiture—black-rimmed frames, white hair, and a black string tie.

Sanders lost his father at a young age and, as he grew, by default, he assumed big responsibilities within his family—including putting food on the table. His early years of work experience served him well and, in his thirties, he was running a restaurant of such renown that it not only became—and remains—a state landmark, but earned him the public rank of Kentucky Colonel. A handful of years later, upon franchising his restaurant, it also earned him hundreds of millions of dollars. And never again was putting food on the table a concern in the Sanders family. When you do those kinds of things, it speaks volumes about you, about your character, and about the unbridled spirit of Kentuckians.

[If needed, use the blank space below then answer the questions.]

- What strategy did you use to retell the story? Why?

- Did your retelling change the story in any way? How?

- How is retelling in this way still a form of imitatio?

(7.3) Narrative

Already you've had a chance to read, reread, analyze, and retell our short narrative. Here you're going to draw on that story again and tell it in a new way, your way. Your task is to, at once, keep the same character in view as well as the same facts, but to tell the story from your own unique perspective. Can you, for instance, tell the story in a funnier, more serious, or even more sad way? Might telling it from a different point of view, say first-person, prove interesting? Choose your vantage point and then your style (comical, serious, etc.) and proceed. Use the space below and/or an extra sheet of paper to compose.

(7.4) Narrative

Just for fun, let's start with a joke. How did the hipster burn his mouth? He ate the pizza before it was cool. Okay, we can't stop there. Here's another: Two gold fish are in a tank. One looks at the other and says, "Hey, you know how to drive this thing?" On a roll, so, one more: What does an angry pepper do when it sees you? It gets jalapeño face! Hopefully you got a laugh from at least one of those. Anyhow, it's time to write.

In this lesson you are to continue practicing imitatio but you now have lots of freedom. This is where you create an original composition. So, enough of Colonel Sanders. Choose someone or something to tell a story about in the genre of non-fiction. (Yes, some stories are quite clearly fiction but here we're imitating the former.) Use the strategy you learned earlier when composing fables:

1. Come up with a setting, knowing that this may take some research;
2. Come up with characters, knowing that this, too, may take some thinking about and perhaps research;
3. Decide on a moral/point;
4. Decide on a plot;
5. Begin writing;
6. Go back through and polish up your language.

Write your answers below in brief and, either on the next page and/or on a separate piece of paper, begin writing.

1. Setting:
2. Characters:
3. Moral/Point:
4. Plot:

(7.4) Narrative

[Use the blank space below and/or additional paper for composing.]

(7.5) Narrative

As with Lesson 6.5, your assignment here is to write a sequel. It will be a sequel to your original composition in in 7.4. Thus, you'll use the same characters but you are free to add other characters, change the setting and point, etc. It's up to you. If you need some ideas for getting started, look back at 6.5 for some suggestions. If not, get to it. Use the space below and/or an additional sheet of paper for your composition.

(8.1) Chreia

Although we have fables and narratives added to our compositional repertoires, we still have much room for other tools and techniques. At this point, we introduce ourselves to Chreia (spelled like Chria by some): "Hello, Chreia. So nice to meet you." Chreia is a Greek word that is related to the English term "saying" but goes beyond it. A chreia, in fact, is really an expounding upon or an exegesis of a saying.

Since pretty much every culture in the world has its own maxims or aphorisms and they are often context-specific, they often need to be explained. This is especially the case for foreigners but even natives often need explanations. When you read the New Testament, for instance, Jesus often has short pithy sayings that his listeners appear to get. Yet, his closest followers are often in-the-dark about the meanings and ask for explanations.

In English, sayings like "It's raining cats and dogs" makes little sense to foreigners. Why, because they take it literally in lieu of having the necessary cultural cues to make sense of it. In some ways, the chreia reminds me of a sermon. Preachers often work with a small chunk of verses and spend time explaining their meaning and significance. When they do this they are engaging in the rhetorical device of amplificatio (i.e. amplification).

Ancient orators like Aphthonius provided some tips on composing chreia and also offered their own examples. Drawing on the work of Matsen, Rollins, and Sousa,[10] I turn our attention to those tips here: 1) Begin with praise for the speaker/author of the saying; 2) Paraphrase the saying; 3) Provide causes or reasons for the saying; 4) Offer a contrasting saying; 5) Give a comparative point or saying; 6) Provide an example that supports the saying; 7) Cite an authority whose testimony proves the saying; and 8) Close with a pointed epilogue.

---

[10] Patricia Matsen, Philip Rollins, and Marion Sousa, *Readings from Classical Rhetoric* (Carbondale: Southern Illinois Press, 1990), 268-9.

What follows is a Hawaiian proverb and my amplification of it: "O ke aloha ka mea i oi aku ka maikai mamua o ka umeke poi a me ka ipukai ia." When translated into English, the result is: "Aloha is far greater than the poi dish."[11] Again, to an outsider, this may seem quite like an odd saying. Yet, the following chreia I have created aims to offer clarification. I use the eight steps previously provided in my chreia. (Note: *Since there is no clearly defined author of this saying, I have chosen to begin by praising Hawaiian culture itself.*)

Aloha is far greater than the poi dish.

(**Praise**) *To the uninitiated, to those deprived of any firsthand experience with the beauty and richness that is Hawaiian culture, I can only say, "I wish it were not so." For this very culture, rooted itself in ancient Polynesian customs and history, has firmly caught me in its grasp and, like a second wind of life gifted from CPR, it has breathed its living spirit into me and lavished its aloha upon me.*

(**Paraphrase**) *And while it is certainly true that we must nourish our bodies, the Hawaiians have taught me that nourishing the spirits of others, as well as my own spirit, is of far greater importance.*

(**Cause/Reason**) *It is often remarked that poi, garnered from the fertile kalo (or: taro) patches of Hawai'i, is a "staple food" of the*

---

[11] Here, I have drawn on the translation of H. L. Sheldon, "Some Hawaiian Proverbs," *Hawaiian Almanac and Annual* (1883): 52-58. His rendering is: "Love is far greater than the poi dish." I have modified his translation, however, in one regard: I have opted to retain the Hawaiian term "aloha," rather than the use the English term "love." I have chosen to do this because it seems to me that "aloha" has a meaning that is, at once, more context-specific than the generic English term "love" and broader than it. Moreover, it is a term that has changed over time. On this and some background to what seems to be the original context of the term, which is what I opt for here, see the work of George H. Kanahele and George S. Kanahele, *Ku Kanaka Stand Tall: A Search for Hawaiian Values* (Honolulu: University of Hawaii Press, 1992), 467-94.

culture. Poi is to Hawai'i what rice is to Indonesia, injera is to Ethiopia, and potatoes are to Germany. For many Hawaiians, poi is their first solid food as a baby. For many Pacific islanders, life without poi is simply unimaginable; indeed, the body seems to demand it. Yet, if the spirit be greater than the body, then how much more is the need for aloha—the basis of the first familial bond born between a child and parents and the communal promise to always sacrifice and look out for one another ahead of oneself?

(Contrast) *Imagine an island replete with taro. Taro on the banks, in the lowlands, spread across the highlands—taro everywhere you look. In this land nobody is at want for the staple food—there is an everlasting abundance and, thus, no worries about eating. And imagine that on this same island there was no aloha. Instead, everyone here seeks his own good at the cost of others, every person is left to fend for himself or herself, and you are constantly looking over your shoulder because no one cares whether you're alive or not. Now, in your estimation, which is greater: aloha or poi?*

(Comparison) *The one striving after aloha, that one's strivings are not in vain because he lives and moves and has his being with others at the fore of his mind. The one seeking to embody aloha is like a mother who first embraces, nurtures, and cares for her child and only then proceeds to feed it. Aloha comes first.*

(Example) *Recently, I witnessed aloha when a group of students at a school in Hawai'i collected 95 bags of supplies for another group of students whom they had never met—and likely never will—on the other side of the globe in Africa. They were seizing the present moment, looking out for others, and displaying a deep reverence for humanity and the human condition. They could have withheld the supplies, keeping them for themselves. Or they could have gathered and sent them begrudgingly. Instead, they embodied and enacted aloha and the intent was, perhaps, greater than the deed itself.*

(**Testimony**) *Jesus Christ once said, "A person cannot live on bread alone, but on every word that proceeds from the mouth of God." For him and his Middle-Eastern compatriots and audience members, bread, too, was a staple food. Yet, he knew that bread alone could not suffice; he knew that there was something greater to look toward. In a like manner, we look to the great truth that "Aloha is greater than the poi dish." Aloha is a necessity of life.*

(**Epilogue**) *Now, my friends, you have encountered, even if only briefly, the essence of Hawaiian culture. And, so, in the spirit of aloha, let's sit together and enjoy a nice dish of poi relishing in the fact that we know which is greater but recognizing that when they're together, it's a beautiful thing.*

So, there you have it, a newborn chreia directly before your eyes. Don't marvel too long, however, because your turn to write one is coming. But the matter at hand now is to simply analyze what you've just read. That, of course, requires looking at it once again. In order to help guide you through that process, simply answer the following (easy) questions below. And once you've done that, please define the terms "amplificatio" and "chreia" and add your definitions to the glossary at the back of the book.

- As a piece of literature, is the preceding chreia convincing? Why or why not?

Amplificatio:

Chreia:

(8.2) Chreia

In this lesson and the next, your goal is to analyze one of two chreia, both taken from the New Testament, and simply break them up into their constituent parts. To that end, in this lesson and the next, both sections (my translations from the Greek) are included with the accompanying verse numbers. I have made it just a tad bit challenging by not including any paragraph breaks. Thus, your job is to write the verse numbers that match the corresponding parts of a chreia in the box that follows. Have fun![12]

1 Timothy 1:2-20

2 To Timothy, a genuine child in faith: grace, mercy, and peace from God the Father and the Anointed One, Jesus, our Lord. 3 Just as I urged you in Ephesus, continue staying in Macedonia in order that you would command certain ones neither to teach otherwise 4 nor to be devoted to myths and endless genealogies, which are about speculations rather than stewardship from God in faith. 5 Moreover, the end of your command is love from a clean heart and a good conscience and a sincere faith, 6 while some certain ones, after they have strayed, wandered into empty discussion, 7 while desiring to be law-teachers, not understanding neither what they are saying nor about the things they are asserting. 8 Well, we know that the law is good if someone makes lawful use of it, 9 seeing this, that for the righteous one the law is not set down, but for the lawless ones and the disobedient ones, the ungodly ones and sinners, for the unholy and profane ones, for the father-abusers and mother-abusers, for man-slaughterers, 10 for the sexually immoral ones, for homosexuals, for man-enslavers, lairs, swindlers, and whatever

---

[12] PS: My outline for this one and the one in the next chapter are in the first footnote of 8.4. Do not, however, use this is a cheat sheet.

thing is otherwise and set up in place of healthy teaching, 11 according to the Gospel of glory of the blessed God, with which I have been entrusted. 12 I thank the one who has strengthened me, the Anointed One, Jesus, our Lord, because he judged me faithful, placing me in service, 13 while formerly being a blasphemer and persecutor and insolent but, I received mercy, because I did it in a lack of faith; 14 moreover, it overflowed, the grace of our Lord, with faithfulness and love which is in the Anointed One, Jesus. 15 Faithful is this word and fully worthy of acceptance: the Anointed One, Jesus, came into the world to save sinners—I myself being first, 16 but on account of this mercy, in order that in me, the first, the Anointed One, Jesus, might put on display his never-ending patience to those who would believe on him for everlasting life. 17 Moreover, to the King of the Ages, (the King) Immortal, (the King) Invisible, to the Only God, honor and glory into the ages of ages. Amen. 18 This is the command I place before you, child Timothy, according to the things professed about you, that in warfare, by them you (be) a good soldier, 19 holding to the faith and a good conscience, which certain ones, while rejecting it, have shipwrecked the faith, 20 some being Hymenaeus and Alexander, whom I have handed to Satan that they would learn not to blaspheme.

Key Elements	Corresponding Verse Numbers
Praise	
Paraphrase	
Cause/Reason	
Contrast	
Comparison	
Example	
Testimony	
Epilogue	

(8.3) Chreia

As you did in 8.2, analyze and dissect the following chreia taken from the New Testament. In the box following the passage of Scripture below, write the verses that go with each of the key elements of the chreia.

2 Timothy 1:2-18

2 To Timothy, beloved child: grace, mercy, peace from God the Father and the Anointed One, Jesus, our Lord. 3 I thank God, whom I worship from of my ancestors with a clean conscience, as I without ceasing, remember about you in my prayers night and day. 4 While longing to see you, remembering your tears, so that I might be filled with joy, 5 I am reminded of your sincere faith, which dwelt first in your grandmother, Lois, and your mother, Eunice; moreover, I am sure that is also in you. 6 Because of this, I remind you to stoke the gift of God, which is in you through the laying on of my hands, 7 for God did not give us a spirit of timidity, but of power and love and self-control. 8 Therefore, neither be ashamed of the witness of our Lord nor of me, his prisoner, but share the suffering in the Gospel according to the power of God, 9 the one who saved us and called us to a holy calling, not according to our works but according to his own purpose and grace, which he gave us in the Anointed One, Jesus, before the ages. 10 Moreover, it has now been revealed through the appearance of our Savior, Jesus, the Anointed One. Further, on the one hand, while abolishing death is bringing forth (grace), on the other hand, life and light through the Gospel, 11 for which I myself was placed a preacher and apostle and teacher. 12 For this reason and these things I am suffering, but I am not ashamed, for I know whom I have believed, and I have become convinced that he is able, the thing set before me, to guard until that day. 13 Follow the pattern of healthy words which, from me, you heard in faith and love that are in the Anointed One, Jesus. 14 The good thing set before (us), guard on account of the Holy Spirit, who deposits (it) in us. **15** *You know this, that they deserted me, all those who are in Asia, some being Phygelus and Hermogenes.* **16** *May the Lord give mercy to Onesiphorus's house, because many times he cared for me, and my chains, he was not ashamed of.* **17** *But while arriving in Rome, he searched earnestly for me and he found (me).* **18** *May the Lord give to him (the opportunity) to find peace from the Lord on that day. And that service he did in Ephesus, you know well (about it).*

Key Elements	Corresponding Verse Numbers
Praise	
Paraphrase	
Cause/Reason	
Contrast	
Comparison	
Example	
Testimony	
Epilogue	

(8.4) Chreia

In this lesson, the goal is for you to compose an original chreia of your own.[13] As for topics, they are wide open—you can write about whatever you choose. If, however, you need some ideas, here you go: healthy eating, gun control, private education, music, and college funding. Use the eight key elements to shape your outline: Praise, Paraphrase, Cause/Reason, Contrast, Comparison, Example, Testimony, and Epilogue. Use the remainder of white space on this page and the next, as well as an extra sheet of paper, if needed.

---

[13] Here are my divisions for the chreia in 8.2 and 8.3. For 1 Tim 1:2-20 the divisions are Praise (2), Paraphrase (3-4), Cause/Reason (5-7), Contrast & Comparison grouped together (8-11), Example (12-14), Testimony (15-17), and Epilogue (18-20). And for 2 Tim 1:2-18 they are: Praise (2-3), Paraphrase (4-5), Cause/Reason (6-7), Contrast (8-9), Comparison (10-11), Example (12-14), Testimony (15-17), and Epilogue (18).

(8.4) Chreia

[Use the blank space below and/or additional paper for composing.]

(8.5) Chreia

As with Lessons 6.5 and 7.5, your assignment here is to write a sequel. It will be a sequel to your original composition in in 8.4. But there is one catch: it needs to be a predominantly negative chreia. So, instead of starting with Praise as the first key element, for example, start with Criticism. Everything else should remain the same but just written with a negative tint: Paraphrase, Cause/Reason, Contrast, Comparison, Example, Testimony, and Epilogue. Use the remainder of white space on this page and the next as well as an extra sheet of paper if needed.

[Use the blank space below and/or additional paper for composing.]

(9.1) Proverb

Every culture and society in the world has proverbs; indeed, they're interestingly human things. Usually, they come in short form, are witty, and seek to persuade their audience. Recently, for instance, I saw a billboard that read: "All people are created equal. All pizzas are not." Can you guess what type of establishment was running this ad? Yep, a pizzeria! (I know, you probably said "a pizza restaurant" because, really, who says "pizzeria"!?)

That was a proverb. It was seeking to persuade readers to forget other pizza joints and to visit theirs instead. It used a bit of humor, was short, catchy, and to-the-point. Moreover, it utilized contrast to make its point. Note that it started with what many would regard as a common truth (i.e. All people are created equal.). It used that as an attention-getter. Then it negated that but it did so in a trivial way that did not *fully* negate the first statement; rather, it was able to use negation in a contrastive way.

The Bible, as you may know, is full of proverbs. In fact, the author of 2 Peter, in 2:22, a section discussing the demise of false teachers, quotes two ancient proverbs. It says, "Of them (i.e. the false teachers) the proverbs are true: 'A dog returns to its vomit,' and, 'A pig that is washed goes back to her wallowing in the mud.'" The first of these is a citation of the Old Testament passage Prov 26:11 and the second, perhaps, is from an ancient book of proverbs often titled Ahiqar. According to scholar Douglas J. Moo, this Semitic proverb, preserved in Aramaic, reads:[14]

My son, you have been to me like the pig who went into the hot bath with people of quality, and when it came out of the hot bath, it saw a filthy hole and it went down and wallowed in it.

---

[14] Douglas J. Moo, "James" in *Hebrews to Revelation* (ZIBBC 4; Grand Rapids: Zondervan, 2002), 50.

Proverbs can take many forms. They can take the form of a pointed statement, a command, a simile, a rhetorical question, etc. All of these can be found in the book of the Bible titled...wait for it...Proverbs. Here are some examples, as you read, notice the distinctive use of contrast:

A pointed statement: "The fear of the Lord is the beginning of knowledge, but fools despise wisdom and instruction" (Prov 1:7);

A command: "My son, if sinful people entice you, do not give in to them" (Prov 1:10);

A simile: "I will mock you when calamity overtakes you, overtakes you like a storm" (Prov 1:26-27); and,

A rhetorical question: "Can a man walk on hot coals without his feet being scorched?" (Prov 6:28)

One of the major foci of proverbs, especially from biblical literature, is wisdom. This is why many scholars refer to a book like Proverbs as "Wisdom Literature." The use of contrast, as noted above, demonstrates that, in this life, pursuing wisdom is often difficult and conflict-laden. As Richard J. Clifford says, "Though wisdom is a free gift, the way to it is through discipline, which is the willingness to learn from others and the capacity to bear pain and contradiction. One acquires wisdom by making oneself open to receive it as a gift."[15]

An important element of understanding proverbs, whether from the Bible or not, is to understand the context or contexts in which they were created. While there is often a rush to view and handle proverbs from the Bible, for instance, as timeless truths rather than timely truths, this can be problematic.

---

[15] Richard J. Clifford, *Proverbs: A Commentary* (OTL; Louisville: WJK, 1999), 33.

For instance, Prov 16:15 says the following: "When a king's face brightens, it means life; his favor is like a rain cloud in spring." For starters, notice the contrast here. See it? The contrast is light and darkness. As Michael V. Fox notes, "This [rain] is the last precipitation until the fall and is crucial to the cereal harvest. There is a certain paradox in identifying the king's favor with both light and the grayness of a rainy day." In Hebrew, the word denotes "a dense rain cloud that produces darkness." For the author of Proverbs, often named Qohelet, "It suggests darkness and gloom."

Second, it is important to recognize that many cultures do not have kings. Simply substituting the leader of one's nation could create a number of problems. For example, changing this to "president," really makes little sense: "When a president's face brightens, it means life; his favor is like a rain cloud in spring." The role of the President of the United States has little similarity to an ancient king.

Third, one must recognize the agrarian tint of this passage. Talk of the rain cloud in spring is one thing but realizing that, in this context, it specifically is referring to a last spring rain that is crucial for the cereal harvest ,is significant. Further, in antiquity, kings often had control over all the land. In the same way that nature could withhold rain and ruin a crop, thus starving its people, a king could snatch up the land and do the same. In short, a king could ruin his subjects' lives.

Yet, a king, particularly an unselfish king who put his people first, is refreshing and celebrated by them. Such a king will be praised and thanked by the people, just as they praise and thank nature when it freely gives of itself to care for them. But the real point, I think, is more of a theological one. In the biblical proverbs, earthly kings are often used as examples to put on display the attributes of the King of kings—God.

Early in Prov 16, for instance, we read, "The lips of a king speak as an oracle, and his mouth doesn't betray justice" (16:10), "Kings detest wrongdoing, for a throne is established through righteousness" (16:12), and "Kings take pleasure in honest lips; they value persons who speak what is right" (16:13). Or: "A king's wrath is a messenger of death, but the wise will appease it" (16:14). While all of these have as their surface focus earthly kings, they are speaking, too, and perhaps even more so, about God the King.

In fact, the earthly kings should look to God the King as their exemplar. Thus, their lips should not betray an oracle because, well, God the King is honest and keeps his word. Likewise, they should be pleased with honest lips because God himself is. Back to our focal proverb, then, the point is that God is the giver of life and death. If one chooses a path toward divine wrath, they'll find it. If, however, they wisely choose the path toward divine life, they'll find it.

God's face is the light toward which we walk, it is what guides us in wisdom and gives us life. God's favor refreshes and restores us and, even more, like an end-of-season rain cloud, it sustains us not only through the storm but the drought, too. To arrive at this type of point took some work but it was worth it. It was worth not forcing our own understanding upon the text and making the Bible say something it never intended to. It was worth maintaining our integrity as interpreters and, in fact, it felt like there was a little bit more payoff by doing it this way. The point: Strive to understand each proverb in its own context, whether modern or ancient.

With that in mind, your task at this point is to read Proverbs 22:17-29. This is a section of Proverbs that, right smack in the middle of the chapter, begins a section of "sayings" (i.e. proverbs). As you read, analyze what you're reading. Do so by looking at each "saying" for the following a) contrast, b) ancient imagery, c) imagery that is uncommon in your everyday life, d) how the proverbs are structured individually, and e) how they fit together as a single entity and/or what they might have in common. On the remainder of this page, as well as the next, analyze the first six "sayings" identifying whether the elements in the list above (i.e. a-e) are present.

(9.1) Proverb

[Use the blank space below and/or additional paper for composing.]

(9.2) Proverb

In Lesson 9.1 you read several proverbs from the Old Testament. Those proverbs came in several forms: a pointed statement, a command, a simile, and a rhetorical question. In addition to these varying forms, you also considered how context should come to bear on the proverbs we encounter and seek to interpret. You also analyzed a portion of Proverbs, paying special attention to a) contrast, b) ancient imagery, c) imagery that is uncommon in your everyday life, d) how the proverbs are structured individually, and e) how they fit together as a single entity.

In this lesson the goal is to get more practice analyzing a portion of Proverbs. In particular, the goal is to focus on Prov 23:1-35, which comprises "sayings" 7-19. You should reword each of the sayings using modern verbiage. In short, put each of the sayings in your own words. Remember, however, to try to understand the context rather than simply making the proverbs sound Americanized or Westernized. There's one catch: your reworded proverbs still need to sound like proverbs! The space for you to rewrite the proverbs has been provided on the following pages. Okay, get to it. Have fun.

Saying 7:

Saying 8:

Saying 9:

Saying 10:

Saying 11:

Saying 12:

Saying 13:

Saying 14:

Saying 15:

Saying 16:

Saying 17:

Saying 18:

Saying 19:

(9.3) Proverb

     Imitate sayings 20-30 found in Prov 24:1-22. You are not going to simply rewrite them; rather, you are going to take the general theme and form of each saying and create your own. Thus, if Saying 21 is about wisdom and it uses a contrast, you should, too, when you compose yours. If Saying 22 is about winning a battle and uses a rhetorical question, you should also write about winning a battle and use a rhetorical question. The aim, however, is to come up with your own proverb. To reiterate: you are not rewriting the proverb, you are simply imitating it. You are mimicking its theme and form and coming up with your own. Go ahead and get started.

Saying 20:

Saying 21:

Saying 22:

Saying 23:

Saying 24:

Saying 25:

Saying 26:

Saying 27:

Saying 28:

Saying 29:

Saying 30:

(9.4) Proverb

In the previous three lessons you worked at analyzing, rewording, and imitating both the structure and content of proverbs taken from the Bible. In this lesson your objective is to use those skills to create your own set of a dozen proverbial sayings. In this exercise, these sayings should be connected via an overarching theme of your choice. Use the space below on this and the next page to compose.

Saying 1:

Saying 2:

Saying 3:

Saying 4:

Saying 5:

Saying 6:

Saying 7:

Saying 8:

Saying 9:

Saying 10:

Saying 11:

Saying 12:

(9.5) Proverb

In Lesson 9.4 you created a dozen original proverbs linked together by an overarching theme. I wish I could read them. Aww, too bad. Hopefully, you were able to share them with someone. In this lesson the task before you is to, once again, come up with a dozen proverbs. This time, however, the proverbs should not be linked together via an overarching theme; instead, you need to create a dozen stand-alone entries. I would suggest that you come up with twelve topics to write about first and then begin creating the proverbs—this will make things easier for you in the long run. And…you're off to the races! Enjoy.

Saying 1:

Saying 2:

Saying 3:

Saying 4:

Saying 5:

Saying 6:

Saying 7:

Saying 8:

Saying 9:

Saying 10:

Saying 11:

Saying 12:

(10.1) Confirmatio & Refutatio

In Lesson 5.3 you learned about the confirmatio (sometimes referred to as the probatio), the part of a work that brings out proofs to substantiate previously offered claims in the propositio and/or partitio. Likewise, in Lesson 5.4 you learned that the refutatio, which also appears in the propositio and/or partitio, is the point where an author or speaker refutes someone's claims. If the speech is given as a response, the aim is to refute what has already been said. Yet, the refutatio can have a preemptive function, too; it can attempt to refute anticipated challenges.

Let's focus here on the confirmatio and, in 10.4 and 10.5, on the refutatio. According to the ancient author, Aphthonius, who wrote a treatise on the progymnasmata, the confirmatio had the following elements, skewed, of course, to the rhetorical situation:

1) The Good Reputation of the Claimant
2) An Exposition of the Matter
3) The Use of the Following Contrastive Headings
    a) Credible Versus not Credible
    b) Possible Versus Impossible
    c) Logical Versus Illogical
    d) Appropriate Versus Inappropriate
    e) Suitable Versus Unsuitable.[16]

Here we'll follow Aphthonius's lead. That is, we'll look at a portion of text containing a confirmation in order to analyze whether it contains the elements listed in steps 1-3. Remember: the confirmation appears in the propositio and/or partitio and offers proofs to substantiate previous claims. As such, it is oftentimes going to be the larger chunk of a text or speech.

---

[16] See George A. Kennedy, *Progymnasmata: Greek Textbooks of Prose Competition and Rhetoric* (WGW 10; Atlanta: Society of Biblical Literature, 2003), 104.

A sample confirmatio that I'd like to focus attention on appears in the New Testament in 1 Cor 15. Interestingly, biblical scholar, Duane Watson, parses the fifteenth chapter of Paul's epistle this way: [17]

exordium (15:1-2),
narratio (15:3-11),
confirmatio and refutatio (15:12-57),
peroratio (15:58).

Even more, he divides 15:12-57 into two discrete units of confirmatio and refutatio. The first unit consists of the following:

refutatio (15:12-19),
confirmatio (15:20-28),
peroratio (15:29-34).

The second unit is structured as follows:

refutatio (15:35-44a),
first portion of the confirmatio (15:44b-49),
second portion of the confirmatio (15:50-57).

If Watson is correct, and he may well be, then Paul certainly wasn't keen on using the approach laid out by Aphthonius. (I am aware, of course, that Aphthonius lived hundreds of years after Paul and that there is no way the Apostle would have been using Aphthonius's work. Instead, I am simply suggesting that the idea about the structure of the confirmatio elaborated on in the later work of Aphthonius may have been available to Paul earlier, just as it may have been available to many others.) If this was, in fact, the case,

---

[17] Duane F. Watson, "Paul's Rhetorical Strategy in 1 Corinthians 15," in *Rhetoric and the New Testament: Essays from the 1992 Heidelberg Conference*, eds. S.E. Porter and T.H. Olbricht (LNTS; JSNTSS 90; T&T Clark, 2001), 248-49.

then we may find the structure spoken of by Aphthonius available in Paul's work. I think this may have been the case. In my view, a case could be made that 1 Cor 15:1-57 has the following order:

1) The Good Reputation of the Claimant (15:1-11)
2) An Exposition of the Matter (15:12-13)
3) The Use of the Following Contrastive Headings
    a) Credible Versus not Credible (15:14-15a)
    b) Possible Versus Impossible (15:15b-28)
    c) Logical Versus Illogical (15:29-34)
    d) Appropriate Versus Inappropriate (15:35-49)
    e) Suitable Versus Unsuitable (15:50-58).

At this point, your job is to analyze 1 Cor 15 and determine whether, in your estimation, either of the above analyses work. If so, which one? (Both cannot be chosen.) If neither, why? Would you divide the text differently? Below, I offer my translation of 1 Cor 15 for you to use.

1 I make known to you, moreover, the Gospel which I announced to you, which you also received and on which you stand,
2 by which you are also saved—this word I kept announcing to you, if you hold to it you have believed, otherwise you would not hold.
3 For I passed on to you in the first place what I also received, this: The Anointed One died for our sins according to the scriptures,
4 and that he was buried, and that he was raised on the third day according to the scriptures,
5 and that he appeared to Cephas, then to the twelve.
6 Then he appeared to more than five hundred siblings at once, out of those many remain until now, but some have fallen asleep.
7 Then he appeared to James, then to all the apostles.
8 Moreover, lastly of all, as one unworthy, he appeared even to me.
9 For I myself am the least of the apostles, which I am not worthy to be called 'apostle,' because I persecuted the church of God;

10 but, by the grace of God, I am what I am, and his grace which is in me has not occurred in vain, but even more than all of them I labored—well, not I, but the grace of God with me.

11 Therefore, then, whether I or those ones, in this manner I preached and in this manner you believed.

12 If, moreover, if it is preached that The Anointed One out from among the dead ones was raised, how are they saying among you, some of them, that there is no resurrection of the dead ones?

13 Moreover, if there is no resurrection of the dead ones, neither has The Anointed One been raised.

14 But if The Anointed One has not been raised, then our preaching is vain and your faith is vain,

15 we are found, moreover, even to be false witnesses of God because we witnessed according to God that, he raised The Anointed One, which if he did not raise, then the dead ones are not raised.

16 For if the dead ones are not raised, neither is The Anointed One raised.

17 Moreover, if The Anointed One is not raised, your faith is useless—still, you are in your sins.

18 Then also, those sleeping in The Anointed One are destroyed.

19 If, in this life, in The Anointed One we are hoping only, pitiful are we of all peoples.

20 Now, moreover, The Anointed One has been raised from the dead ones, the firstfruit of those sleeping.

21 For, since through men death (came), also through a man resurrection from the dead ones (comes).

22 For just as in Adam all die, so also in The Anointed One all are made alive.

23 Further, each in his own way: the firstfruit is The Anointed one, then those of The Anointed One in his royal (re)entry.

24 Then the last, when he shall hand over the kingdom of God even to the Father, whenever he destroys every ruler and every authority and power,

25 for he must rule until which he shall put all enemies under his feet.

26 The last enemy to be destroyed is death,

27 for everything he put under his feet. Well, when it is said that "everything is put under," clearly this is outside the one putting all things under him.

28 Moreover, whenever, he put all things under him, then this same son will be put under by the one putting all things under him so that God is all in all.

29 So why are some of the ones baptized are doing this on account of "the dead ones." If the whole of the dead ones is not raised, why are they even being baptized on account of them?

30 Why also are we endangering ourselves every hour?

31 Daily I die, yes, I boast about you, which I have in The Anointed One, Jesus, our Lord.

32 If according to a man I fought wild beasts in Ephesus, to me what's the gain? If the dead ones are not raised, "We shall eat and drink, for tomorrow we die."

33 Do not be deceived, bad companionships corrupt good character.

34 Sober up rightly and do not sin, for some have an ignorance of God. To shame you, I speak.

35 But some of you say, "How are the dead ones raised? Moreover, with what kind of body do they come?"

36 Fool, you, what you sow does not come to life unless it dies.

37 And what you sow is not the to-come body you sow but a naked seed, either a stalk of grain or some other thing.

38 Moreover, God the one who shall give him a body as he is well pleased and each of the seeds its own body.

39 Not all flesh is the same flesh, but one then of men, further, one the flesh of beasts, moreover, one the flesh of birds, additionally, one of fish.

40 Both heavenly bodies and earthly bodies. Further, the other, on the hand, is the glory of the heavenlies, but on the other hand, of the earthlies.

41 One the glory of the son, and one the glory of the moon, and one the glory of the stars, for star from star differs in glory.

42 And in this manner, the resurrection of the dead ones. It is sown in decay, raised in immortality.

43 Sown in dishonor, raised in glory. Sown in weakness, raised in power.

44 Sown a natural body, raised a spiritual body. If it is a natural body, it is also spiritual.

45 Thus it is also written, "He became, the first man, Adam, living in nature; the last Adam was made alive in the Spirit."

46 But not first the spiritual rather the natural, then (came) the spiritual.

47 The first man (came) from out of Earth's dust, the second man out of heaven.

48 The one which was like the dust, those also are of the dust, and the one which was like the heavenly, those also are of the heavenlies.

49 And just like we have taken on the image of the dust, we will also take on the image of the heavenly.

50 Moreover, this I say, siblings, that flesh and blood are not able to inherit the kingdom of God, nor the decay inherit the immortal.

51 Behold the mystery I say to you: We will not all sleep, but we will all be changed.

52 In an instant, in the blink of an eye, on the last trumpet; for will trumpet and the dead ones will be raised imperishable and we will all ourselves be changed.

53 It is necessary for the perishable to be clothed in this, the imperishable, and the mortal to be clothed in this, the immortal.

54 Moreover, when the perishable was clothed in this imperishable and the mortal clothed in this immortal, then it will come to pass, the word written: "Death will be swallowed up in victory."

55 Where of you, death, is victory? Where of you, death, is your bite?

56 Well, sin is the bite of death, but the power of sin is the law;

57 Moreover, thanks be to God, the one giving us the victory through our Lord, Jesus, The Anointed one.

58 So, siblings, my beloved, become steadfast, immovable, abounding in the works of the Lord always, seeing that your labor is not in vain in the Lord.

[Use the blank space below to compose notes and/or other thoughts.]

(10.2) Confirmatio & Refutatio

In this section I want to begin by attempting to use Aphthonius's outline of the confirmation to analyze a portion of a modern speech. This same outline, of course, holds true for the refutatio, which I will discuss in subsequent lessons. So, read the bit below about a recent event in American history, analyze it, critique it, and then answer the question that follows.[18]

1) The Good Reputation of the Claimant

The defendant, Mr. Orenthal James Simpson, is now afforded an opportunity to argue the case, if you will, but I'm not going to argue with you, ladies and gentlemen. What I'm going to do is to try and discuss the reasonable inferences which I feel can be drawn from this evidence. At the outset, let me join with the others in thanking you for the service that you have rendered. You are truly a marvelous jury, the longest-serving jury in Los Angeles County and perhaps the most patient and healthy jury we've ever seen. I hope that your health and your good health continues.

We met approximately one year and one day ago, September 26th, 1994. I guess we've been together longer than some relationships, as it were. But we've had a unique relationship in this matter, in that you've been the judges of the facts. We have been advocates on both sides. The judge has been the judge of the law. We all understand our various roles in this endeavor that I'm going to call a journey toward justice. That's what we're going to be talking about this afternoon as I seek to address you.

The final test of your service as jurors will not lie in the fact that you've stayed here more than a year. It will lie in the quality of the verdict that you render and whether or not that verdict bespeaks justice as a move towards justice. Now you recall, during a process

---

[18] The following transcript was taken from the CNN website. The link was last accessed on 2/1/18 and can be found at www.cnn.com/US/OJ/ daily/9-28/transcripts/trans5.html.

called voir dire examination, each of you were thoroughly questioned by the lawyers. You probably thought, gee, I wish they'd leave me alone. But you understood, I'm sure, that this is very serious business.

2) An Exposition of the Matter

Our client, Mr. Orenthal James Simpson, is on trial for his life.

3) The Use of the Following Contrastive Headings
a) Credible Versus not Credible

And so we had to be very, very careful, both sides, in trying to get people who could be fair to both sides. You will recall those questions that you keep an open mind, which I hope you still have even to this day, that you wouldn't be swayed by sympathy for or passion against either side in this case, that you would give both sides of this lawsuit the benefit of your individual opinion. No one, no one, can tell you what the facts are. That's going to be your job to determine. It's not a question of age or experience. And we talked about that. This is one of those jobs where you kind of learn on the job.

b) Possible Versus Impossible

And so it's important that you fully understand that, and that's why voir dire was so very important as we asked you all of those questions before you were sequestered and before you were actually picked. Now, each of you filled out the questionnaire and you answered the questions honestly, I'm sure. You know, Cicero said long ago that he who violates his oath profanes the divinity of faith itself. And, of course, both sides in this lawsuit have faith that you will live up to your promises, and I'm sure you'll do that.

You know, Abraham Lincoln said that jury service is the highest act of citizenship. So if it's any consolation to you, you've been involved in that very highest act of citizenship. And so, again, we applaud you and we thank you. Let's move toward justice. One other entity or group of ladies, there are two ladies that I should thank, are our marvelous court reporters. They have been patient with us, they've been here from the very beginning, we very much appreciate them in their services, and I especially appreciate them because sometimes I speak rather rapidly and they have tough time keeping up with me. So I trust that today, if I started to speak too fast in my zeal, Ms. Markson [sp] and Chris will bring that to my attention, I'm sure they will.

Now, in the course of this process, what we are discussing the reasonable inferences of the evidence, I ask you to remember that we're all advocates, we're all officers of this court. I will recall the evidence and speak about the evidence. Should I misstate that evidence, please don't hold that against Mr. Simpson. I will never intentionally do that. In fact, I think you'll find that during my presentation, unlike my learned colleagues on the other side, I'm going to read you testimony, what the witnesses actually said, so there'll be no misunderstanding about what was said about certain key things.

But remember that we're all advocates, and I think it was Ms. Clark who said, saying it's so doesn't make it so. I think that applies very much to their arguments. Ultimately, it's what you determine to be the facts. That's what's going to be important, and all of us will live with that. You are empowered to do justice. You are empowered to insure that this great system of ours works.

Listen for a moment, will you please, one of my favorite people in history is the great Frederick Douglass. He said shortly after the slaves were free, quote, `In a composite nation like ours, as before the law there should be no rich, no poor, no high, no low, no white, no black, but common country, common citizenship, equal rights, and a common destiny.' This marvelous statement was made more than 100 years ago. It's an ideal worth striving for and one that we still strive for. We haven't reached this goal yet, but certainly in this great country of ours we're trying. With a jury such as this, we hope we can do that in this particular case.

c) Logical Versus Illogical

Now, in this case, you are aware that we represent Mr. Orenthal James Simpson. The prosecution never calls him Mr. Orenthal James Simpson, they call him defendant. I want to tell you right at the outset that Orenthal James Simpson, like all defendants, is presumed to be innocent. He's entitled to the same dignity and respect as all the rest of us. As he sits over there now, he's cloaked in a presumption of innocence. You will determine the facts of whether or not he's set free to walk out those doors or whether he spends the rest of his life in prison. But he's Orenthal James Simpson, he's not just the defendant. And we on the defense are proud, consider it a privilege to have been part of representing him in this exercise and this journey toward justice. Make no mistake about it.

Finally, I apologize to you for the length that this journey has taken. But you know when you're seeking justice there are no shortcuts. If you were to trade places with either side you'd want someone who'd fight hard for you and vigorously, especially if it was a person who had maintained their innocence from the very beginning of the proceedings. Some of you in voir dire talked about that, that you'd been involved in other cases where you felt the lawyers didn't stand. Well, I certainly hope that in this case on both sides you felt that lawyers did their best to represent their respective position, and we will continue, I'm sure, to do that so that, although I apologize for the length of the trial, I hope and I trust that you will understand that in a journey toward justice there is no shortcut.

d) Appropriate Versus Inappropriate

Finally, with regard to your responsibilities, we asked you at the very beginning to don't compromise. This is not a case for the timid or the weak of heart. This is not a case for the naive. This is a case for courageous citizens who believe in the Constitution. And while I'm talking about the Constitution, think with me for a moment how many times you heard my learned adversaries say, the defense didn't prove, the defense didn't do this, the defense didn't that.

Remember, back in voir dire? What did the judge tell us? Judge Ito said the defense could sit here and do absolutely nothing. One of you is from Missouri and he reminded you who's from Missouri here? Say to the prosecution, you show us. Now, we didn't do that. But we don't have an obligation, as you'll see.

You've heard from the jury instructions and at the end I will show you some others. We don't have to do anything. We don't have to prove anything. This is the prosecution's burden, and we can't let them turn the Constitution on its head. We can't let them get away from their burden. It's my job, one of my jobs, is to remind you of that and to remind them of that, that that's their burden. They must prove Mr. Simpson guilty beyond a reasonable doubt and to a moral certainty, and we will talk about what a reasonable doubt means.

e) Suitable Versus Unsuitable

And so now as we have this opportunity to analyze the facts of the case, I agree with one thing that Mr. Darden said, to this task I ask you to bring your common sense. Collectively, the 14 of you have more than 500 years of experience. I know you're all young but you multiply that 14, you won't hold that against me, I don't think. Five hundred years of experience. You didn't leave your common sense out in that hallway when you came in here, and we're going to ask you to apply it to the facts of this case.

Do you think this "closing statement" fits Aphthonius's model of a confirmatio or does it seemed forced? Explain your response.

(10.3) Confirmatio & Refutatio

The goal of today's lesson is to write a confirmatio. Now, as you know, the confirmatio usually falls within the middle of a speech or essay. Since you have not written an introduction and other portions of a speech to precede this, your job is to simply write the confirmatio. It will still work! Use the three sections as well as the five subsections listed below. Write in the book and/or on some additional paper if you need to.

1) The Good Reputation of the Claimant
2) An Exposition of the Matter
3) The Use of the Following Contrastive Headings
     a) Credible Versus not Credible
     b) Possible Versus Impossible
     c) Logical Versus Illogical
     d) Appropriate Versus Inappropriate
     e) Suitable Versus Unsuitable.

[Use the blank space below and/or additional paper for composing.]

(10.4) Confirmatio & Refutatio

As has already been pointed out several times in this book, the refutatio is the point where an author or speaker refutes someone's claims, whether those claims have already been made or they are simply anticipated. While a confirmatio and refutatio could certainly be mixed to some degree, I have chosen to focus on them as separate entities here in order to gain a clearer understanding of each. Moreover, in ancient rhetorical theory the refutatio was typically viewed as following the confirmatio. So, in this lesson, your job is to read the text below, which is taken from the New Testament text known as Galatians, and decide whether this outline seems correct or not.

In my view, Gal 4:11-6:10 seems to bear the format of a refutatio structured along the lines of what Aphthonius suggested. Of course, orators had much flexibility in antiquity and were often encouraged to mix things up even while adhering to the common standards. While others have asserted that a refutatio exists at different boundaries in Galatians,[19] my demarcation is as follows:

1) The Good Reputation of the Claimant (Gal 4:11-14)
2) An Exposition of the Matter (Gal 4:11-17)
3) The Use of the Following Contrastive Headings
    a) Credible Versus not Credible (4:18-20)
    b) Possible Versus Impossible (4:21-31)
    c) Logical Versus Illogical (5:1-6)
    d) Appropriate Versus Inappropriate (5:7-26)
    e) Suitable Versus Unsuitable (6:1-10)

---

[19] See, for instance, Bernard H. Brinsmead, *Galatians: Dialogical Response to Opponents* (SBLDS 65; Chico, Calif.: Scholars, 1982), esp. 53-67 and James D. Hester, "The Use and Influence of Rhetoric in Galatians 2:1-14," *Theolgische Zeitschrift* 42 (1986): 387-92, who place it from 5:1-6:10. Obviously, this view does not take into consideration the outline later found in Aphthonius.

4:11 I fear on account of you, lest somehow I have wasted efforts on you.

12 Become as I am, because I also am like you; siblings, I plead with you. You haven't persecuted me.

13 Further, you know it was because of the weakness of the flesh, I announced the Gospel to you formerly,

14 and it was a trial to you in my flesh, neither did you consider me a nobody nor did you spit on me but, like an angel of God, you welcomed me like The Anointed One, Jesus.

15 Where, then, is your joy? For I witnessed with you that, if you were able to rip out your eyes, you would have given them to me.

16 And so, have I become your enemy from speaking truth to you?

17 They are zealous for you, not well-intentioned, but they want to alienate you in order that you are zealous for them.

18 Moreover, it is good to be zealous in good always, and not only in the present, me being with you,

19 my children, whom again I am in birth pains for until when The Anointed One makes changes in you.

20 Further, I want to be with you still and to change my tone because I am confused by you.

21 Tell me, those wanting to be under the law, are you not listening to the law?

22 For it is written that Abraham had two sons, one from the female servant and one from the free woman.

23 Well, on the one hand, the one from the female servant was born according to the flesh but, on the other hand, the one from the free woman through a promise.

24 This is an allegory, for these are two covenants; on the one hand, the one from Mt. Sinai, the one born from a servant, this one is Hagar;

25 moreover, Mt. Sinai is Hagar in Arabia; further, it corresponds now to Jerusalem, for she serves with her children.

26 But the Jerusalem above is the free, which is our mother.

27 For it is written: Rejoice, a seed, the one not bearing children, shout and cry, the one not in labor pains, because many are the children of the wilderness, greater than the one having a husband.

28 Well, with me, siblings, according to Isaac's promise, you are children.

29 But also, then, the one born according to the flesh persecuted the one according to the Spirit, so also even now.

30 But what does the scripture say? Expel the female servant and her son, for never will the son of the servant woman inherent with the son of the free woman.

31 Because of this, siblings, we are not children of the servant woman but of the free.

5:1 For freedom, The Anointed One, freed us; therefore, stand and never again put on the yoke of the slave woman.

2 Look, I Paul, I myself say to you this: If you are circumcised, The Anointed One will be of no worth for you.

3 But I witness again to every person being circumcised that he is obligated to do the whole law.

4 You are being separated from The Anointed One, those in the law are seeking justification; from grace you have fallen.

5 For we in the Spirit, through faith, eagerly anticipate the hope of righteousness.

6 For in The Anointed One, Jesus, neither is circumcision something mighty nor is uncircumcision, but faith working through love.

7 You were running well. Did not someone cut you off from the truth to persuade?

8 The persuasion is not from The One Calling you.

9 A little yeast leavens the whole batch of yeast.

10 I myself am persuaded by you in the Lord because no one considers the other. Moreover, the one troubling you will pay for the judgment, whoever that may be.

11 But I, siblings, if I am preaching circumcision, why still am I persecuted? Then the scandal is separated from the cross.

12 I wish even for those standing up before you to be cut off (or: emasculated).

13 For you yourselves were called to be free, siblings, only do not employ freedom for the flesh, but through love serve one another.

14 For all the law in one word is fulfilled, in this: Love your neighbor as yourself.

15 Moreover, if you keep biting and devouring one other, watch, lest by one another you shall be destroyed.

16 Further, I say, walk in the Spirit and the desires of the flesh, never fulfill.

17 For the flesh desires against the Spirit, moreover, the Spirit against the flesh, for these are antithetical to one another in order that you do not do these things that you want.

18 But if you are led by the Spirit, you are not under the law.

19 But the works of the flesh are obvious, these are: sexual immorality, impurity, debauchery,

20 idolatry, drug-induced states, hatred, jealousy, zealotry, selfishness, acts of hatred, double-mindedness, factions,

21 envy, drunkenness, orgies, and things like these, which I am saying to you just as I said before because the ones doing these things will not inherit the kingdom of God.

22 But the fruit of the Spirit is love, joy, peace, longsuffering, kindness, goodness, faithfulness,

23 gentleness, self-control—against these things there is no law.

24 Further, those of The Anointed One crucified the flesh with those passions and desires.

25 If we are living in the Spirit, in the Spirit also let us be principled.

26 Let us not become vainglorious, putting ourselves before others, envying one another.

6:1 Siblings, if also you catch a person in some trespass, you yourselves, the spiritual ones, restore them by the Spirit gently, watching yourself lest also you are tempted.

2 Bear one another's burdens and, in this manner, you will fulfill the law of The Anointed One.

3 For if he thinks himself to be someone when he is not someone, he is deceiving himself.

4 But if each thinks about his own work, even then the boast is only on account of himself and he is not (thinking) on account of the other,

5 for each bears his own load.

6 Well, let the one being instructed share the word with the one teaching on everything good.

7 Do not be deceived, God is not mocked, for that which a person sows, this also he will harvest,

8 because the one sowing in his own flesh, from the flesh he will harvest decay, but the one sowing in the Spirit, from the Spirit he will harvest life everlasting.

9 But the ones doing good, let us not tire, for in due time we will harvest, never quitting.

10 Therefore, then, as we have time, let us work doing good for all, moreover, especially for those of the household of faithfulness.

(10.5) Confirmatio & Refutatio

Now that you have written a confirmatio and have also read a refutatio, your task is to compose an original refutatio. To do this, you will use the same set of headings and subheadings suggested by Aphthonius (given below). Happy writing!

1) The Good Reputation of the Claimant
2) An Exposition of the Matter
3) The Use of the Following Contrastive Headings
    a) Credible Versus not Credible
    b) Possible Versus Impossible
    c) Logical Versus Illogical
    d) Appropriate Versus Inappropriate
    e) Suitable Versus Unsuitable.

[Use the blank space below and/or additional paper for composing.]

(11.1) Commonplace

Earlier in this book you read about how invention is concerned with the ability to draw on a storehouse of common knowledge while also advancing new arguments. Such an act was only possible in antiquity because many orators were systematic in their approach to writing and speaking. For instance, as Fredrick Long has pointed out, in the three species of rhetoric—deliberative, forensic/judicial, and epideictic—there were also accompanying topical concerns.[20]

So, for instance, in a deliberative piece of rhetoric, goodness and utility were often the chief concerns. In judicial/forensic rhetoric justice and injustice were typically in view. And in epideictic rhetoric vice and virtue were at the forefront.[21] Because each species of rhetoric was understood to be able to deal with certain topics, a rhetor could withdraw from this bank of knowledge rather quickly and conveniently.

Thus, there were four *general topoi* required by all orators: a) possibility or impossibility, b) past and future fact, c) greater or lesser degree, and d) amplification and depreciation. In addition, there were three *special topoi*, oriented toward ethics and politics, that rhetors could draw on: a) nature and number of motives, b) the mindset of those acting, and c) the character and dispositions of those exposed to injustice.[22]

In addition to these, Aristotle actually developed twenty-eight types of *formal argumentative topoi* (i.e. topics) for orators to draw from, these are also known as commonplaces. After him, both Quintilian and Cicero said similar things. Below, drawing heavily from Long's notes, I offer Aristotle's list along with identifiers noting where Quintilian and Cicero also identified these

---

[20] Fredrick J. Long, *Ancient Rhetoric and Paul's Apology: The Compositional Unity of 2 Corinthians* (SNTSMS 131; Cambridge: Cambridge University Press, 2004), 66.

[21] Ibid.

[22] Ibid., 65.

commonplaces.[23] It should be noted here, however, that while Cicero and Quintilian addressed some of these same commonplaces, they, too, had their own creative takes on what they were and how to utilize them.[24]

1. Arguments from opposites (cf. Cicero and Quintilian)
2. Arguments from inflections/derivatives (cf. Cicero and Quintilian)
3. Arguments from correlative terms (cf. Cicero and Quintilian)
4. Arguments from more and less (cf. Cicero and Quintilian)
5. Arguments from time (cf. Quintilian)
6. Arguments that turn the opponent's argument against him or her
7. Arguments from definitions (cf. Cicero and Quintilian)
8. Arguments on ambiguous terms
9. Arguments from division (cf. Cicero and Quintilian)
10. Arguments from induction
11. Arguments from existing decisions/authority (cf. Cicero)
12. Arguments from parts to whole (cf. Cicero and Quintilian)
13. Arguments from simple consequences (cf. Cicero and Quintilian)
14. Arguments from crisscrossing (cf. Cicero)
15. Arguments from inward thoughts and outward actions
16. Arguments from proportional results/analogy (cf. Cicero)
17. Arguments from identical results of action/decision
18. Arguments from altered choices
19. Arguments from attributed motives
20. Arguments concerning incentives and deterrents for people

---

[23] The main source material from Aristotle is found in his *Ars Rhetorica* 2.23. For Quintilian, see his *Institutes of Oratory* 5.10.53-91. And for Cicero see his *On Oratory* 2.163-73, *Parts of Oratory* 2.7, and *Topics* 8-25, and 71.

[24] See Richard McKeown, "Creativity and the Commonplace," *Philosophy & Rhetoric* 4 (1973): 208. There he notes, "Cicero's commonplaces are not Aristotle's, Boethius departs beyond both, Lully and Ramus innovate, and Bacon, Leibniz, and Vico refashion their innovations."

21. Arguments from incredible occurrences
22. Arguments from conflicting facts or actions (cf. Cicero)
23. Arguments explaining circumstances/accusations (cf. Cicero)
24. Arguments from cause to effect (cf. Cicero and Quintilian)
25. Arguments for a better course of action
26. Arguments comparing whether actions are contrary
27. Arguments noting previous mistakes
28. Arguments on the meaning of names (cf. Cicero and Quintilian)[25]

It is important to bear in mind that the content associated with these commonplaces is meant to intersect with the present, the novel, and the creative. Richard McKeown refers to them as the "commonplaces of creativity" (see below). I agree. He makes the following statement which, although lengthy, is worth considering:

> *The commonplaces of creativity operate in the interpretation of texts as well as in the writing of texts, in the interpretation of experience as well as of statements, in the interpretation and formation of character, thought, actions, and things. In the interpretation of the text of a philosopher, past or present, commonplaces of invention may open up the perception of new meanings and applications even in a familiar text, which in turn uncovers previously unperceived lines of arguments to unnoticed conclusions which were not there until they were made facts by discovery. The newly perceived facts of interpreting a text may in turn lead to the discovery of new powers of perception and their use in the discovery of new existential data and new experiential facts, set in relation by new arts and methods, to discover new universes of discourse, thought, consequential occurrence, and systematic organization. The use of commonplaces of creativity erects and fills the commonplace as a storehouse of*

---

[25] Long, *Paul's Apology*, 66.

the familiar to provide materials for commonplaces as instruments for the perception, creation, arrangement, and establishment of the new in existence, experience, discursive exploration, and inclusive organization.[26]

So, commonplaces are used to bring the familiar into conjunction with the new. The end-result is the creation of something beautiful, something part tradition and part innovation. If you have ever watched someone who freestyle raps and does it well, this is exactly what they are doing. They use familiar techniques, topics, and imagery but also blend it with something fresh and immediately relevant. And while they're coming up with the arrangement and words on the spot, they're also drawing from a rich storehouse of language and imagery to do so. Even more, it's done quickly and often forcefully, making it immensely impressive.

In that spirit, I am going to try my hand at this below. What follows, then, is an on-the-spot rap I will come up with in a period of three minutes. I did not write this in the past but, right now, I am certainly drawing on a storehouse of knowledge, a storehouse of commonplaces. When you're finished reading whatever is to come, answer the questions that follow.

A Freestyle Rap on Commonplaces

Everywhere I go, I get showered in folks' graces
And everywhere I go, my footsteps are leavin' traces
And everyone I know, yeah, all these familiar faces
They recognize my name, it's become a commonplace, yeah
No, it's not a race man, 'cause I'll outrun 'em all always
I may be thirty-seven but I still got speed for like days
And my rhymes are like fire, heat, hot just like a blaze
They'll burn a hater up just like the sun's rays
And then they'll watch me elevate, see me on the raise

---

[26] McKeown, "Creativity," 209-10.

I'm the Rhetoric King, like Aristotle I amaze
Like Cicero, I flow, I go, I demonstrate, I show
And these rhymes they're loaded with intellect and feelin'
'Cause I'm passionate and eloquent just like Quintilian
And even though I don't make a million
My estate is up high, 'cause I'm one of God's children
So don't mistake me for shy, and don't mistake me as coy
'Cause like Star Wars I bring rhetorical force but I do it with *topoi*

Okay, that actually took 4 minutes not 3. Again, I made it up on the spot but I was drawing on things familiar to me and, hopefully, to you and all who read it. At this point, I haven't even gone back and looked at it yet, but your goal is to do just that as you answer the questions below by giving examples.

1. Does the freestyle rap use any of the *formal argumentative topoi* denoted by Aristotle?

2. Does the freestyle rap use any general imagery that is immediately recognizable, that is, something most people would be familiar with?

3. Does the freestyle rap mix something ancient or traditional with something novel and/or innovative?

4. Does the freestyle rap include any rhetorical moves and/or devices that stand out to you?

(11.2) Commonplace

In the previous lesson, you learned about the notion of the commonplace. You were introduced to various types of *topoi* as well. Near the end of the lesson, you encountered a freestyle rap of mine, one in which I attempted to draw on a storehouse of knowledge that I also wanted to connect with the present. You, dear reader, may be a judge on whether or not I achieved that; but, hopefully you were nice because now it is your turn. You have five minutes to come up with a rap. It doesn't have to be a freestyle but, by virtue of me putting this challenge to you right now, it will have to be in some regard. Your topic to write about is rhetoric and you should try to incorporate some of the commonplaces. Use the space below to compose. 3-2-1...Go!

(11.3) Commonplace

In Lesson 11.1 you were introduced to four *general topoi* required by all orators: a) possibility or impossibility, b) past and future fact, c) greater or lesser degree, and d) amplification and depreciation. In addition, you learned about three *special topoi* oriented toward ethics and politics that rhetors could draw on: a) nature and number of motives, b) the mindset of those acting, and c) the character and dispositions of those exposed to injustice. In this lesson your goal is to get a bit more familiar with these.

Thus, in what follows, your charge is to develop one example of each type. More specifically, write at least one paragraph exemplifying each of these at work. For instance, when dealing with the general *topos* of "possibility or impossibility," create an argument from one of these vantage points while also discounting the other. Begin!

Four General *Topoi*

a) possibility or impossibility

b) past and future fact

c) greater or lesser degree

d) amplification and depreciation.

Three Special *Topoi*

a) nature and number of motives

b) the mindset of those acting

c) the character and dispositions of those exposed to injustice

(11.4) Commonplace

Now that you have reviewed and used the four general *topoi* and the three special *topoi* that were used by ancient orators, it's time to revisit the twenty-eight formal argumentative *topoi*, also known as commonplaces, as denoted by Aristotle. Here, however, you'll only revisit the first fourteen. In this lesson, your aim is similar to that given in 11.3—develop one example of each by composing at least one paragraph.

Fourteen of the Twenty-Eight Formal Argumentative *Topoi*

1. Arguments from opposites (cf. Cicero and Quintilian)

2. Arguments from inflections/derivatives (cf. Cicero and Quintilian)

3. Arguments from correlative terms (cf. Cicero and Quintilian)

4. Arguments from more and less (cf. Cicero and Quintilian)

5. Arguments from time (cf. Quintilian)

6. Arguments that turn the opponent's argument against him or her

7. Arguments from definitions (cf. Cicero and Quintilian)

8. Arguments on ambiguous terms

9. Arguments from division (cf. Cicero and Quintilian)

10. Arguments from induction

11. Arguments from existing decisions/authority (cf. Cicero)

12. Arguments from parts to whole (cf. Cicero and Quintilian)

13. Arguments from simple consequences (cf. Cicero and Quintilian)

14. Arguments from crisscrossing (cf. Cicero)

(11.5) Commonplace

In 11.4 you revisited the first fourteen of Aristotle's twenty-eight formal argumentative *topoi*. Here, in 11.5, you are to work with the last fourteen. Once again, engage each one developing an example argument in the space of a single paragraph. Enjoy!

Fourteen of the Twenty-Eight Formal Argumentative *Topoi*

1. Arguments from inward thoughts and outward actions

2. Arguments from proportional results/analogy (cf. Cicero)

3. Arguments from identical results of action/decision

4. Arguments from altered choices

5. Arguments from attributed motives

6. Arguments concerning incentives and deterrents for people

7. Arguments from incredible occurrences

8. Arguments from conflicting facts or actions (cf. Cicero)

9. Arguments explaining circumstances/accusations (cf. Cicero)

10. Arguments from cause to effect (cf. Cicero and Quintilian)

11. Arguments for a better course of action

12. Arguments comparing whether actions are contrary

13. Arguments noting previous mistakes

14. Arguments on the meaning of names (cf. Cicero and Quintilian

(12.1) Encomium & Invective

In Lesson 4.3 you learned about the encomium and its counterpart, the invective. Stated simply, an encomium is a word of praise about someone or something and an invective (also known as vituperation) is a word of blame or criticism. When crafting either of these, as Jerome Neyrey has pointed out and which I cite in full below, the ancients had a generic format that one could follow. This format was situated between an exordium and epilogue:

(Exordium)
I. Origin
    a. Geography and Generation: country, race, ancestors, parents
    b. Birth: phenomena at birth (stars, visions, etc.), oracles
II. Nurture and Training
    a. Education: teachers, arts, skills, laws, mode of life
III. Accomplishments
    a. Deeds of the Body: beauty, strength, agility, might, health
    b. Deeds of the Soul: justice, wisdom, temperance, courage, piety
    c. Deeds of Fortune: power, wealth, friends, fame, fortune
IV. Comparison
V. Noble Death and Posthumous Honors.[27]
(Epilogue)

This outline provides a more in-depth way of approaching and analyzing an encomium than you encountered in Lesson 4.3. Your task at present is to keep this in mind as you read the following

---

[27] Jerome H. Neyrey, "Encomium vs. Vituperation: Contrasting Portraits of Jesus in the Fourth Gospel," in *The Gospel of John in Cultural and Rhetorical Perspective* (Grand Rapids: Eerdmans, 2009), 7.

encomium, which is about the Cincinnati Bengals—a team in the National Football League from my birth state, Ohio. This, in fact, is what we might call a mock encomium since it allows sarcasm to masquerade as praise and is not quite a vituperation in the technical sense of the term.

An Encomium to the Cincinnati Bengals

(Exordium)

As consistent as a bowel movement after a visit to Taco Bell, you, O' Cincinnati Bengals, grace the August gridiron with your presence. How lucky, how lucky are we, your longsuffering fans!

I. Origin

Nestled along the Ohio River, you guard our lair, The Jungle, defending her fiercely...sometimes. Each fall, you make The Queen City dream...of what it might be like to root for another team. Your forefather, Paul Brown, birthed you in 1966 and, in your fifty-year-plus tenure, like an absentee parent, you have not failed to disappoint the many boys and girls who have given up years of their lives admiring you. At a minimum, you have gifted your Ohio-proud fans with the ability to say, "At least we don't have to cheer for the Cleveland Browns." Perhaps, best of all, you have handed down for all generations "The Ickey Shuffle."

II. Nurture and Training

You have taught us well what it means to be a student of the game...of losing well. Losing with grace and humility, as you have shown us, is an art form; it takes skill. It is a skill that has been perfected by your fan base throughout the decades. When you went to the Super Bowl in both 1981 and 1988, we were beside ourselves. When you lost, well, we just want you to know that the gaping hole of depression that the city spiraled into was not really your fault. In no way, shape, or form does it sit in the back of our minds and resurface at the start of each season...except the opposite.

III. Accomplishments

We admire how you, as individual players, have sacrificed for us. Indeed, you have sacrificed our pride, our spirit, and our hope. Watching you play on any given Sunday is truly a call for us to sacrifice, too—our health and money. You, dearest Bengals, you have soul. You are courageous when you step onto the field. Toward your opponents you display temperance in effort and unselfishness in wins. Your fortune is mesmerizing. The way you fill the stands year after year resembles the beauty of a magician's sleight of hand.

IV. Comparison

I ask you, my dear Bengals, who else in the NFL would be so fortunate to have Coach Lewis at the helm? Perhaps the New England Patriots who, under the leadership of Bill Belichick, have won five Super Bowls? Probably not. Or what about on the roster of our rivals, the Pittsburgh Steelers, who are also among the winningest teams in Super Bowl history? Not sure there'd be much of a welcome there! Well, what about in San Francisco with the 49ers, the team who has reigned victorious over us in our two Super Bowl appearances? Perhaps.

V. Noble Death and Posthumous Honors

Dearest Bengals, to whom much has been given, much is expected. Sure, you have been bestowed with numerous arrests by the Cincinnati PD, but we would rather read and hear news about winning titles rather than battery, drunk driving, or being in possession of illegal substances. Let's bring some honor to the orange, white, and black; let's drop the Ochcinco-type shenanigans; and, let's make Boomer and Collinsworth proud alumnae.

(Epilogue)

I, with my sons and daughters, wait for the day when we return to the Super Bowl. Indeed, we are waiting together for that win. We are waiting again for the day when we can proudly and confidently respond to the inquisitive chant, "Who dey, who dey, who dey think gonna' beat 'dem Bengals?" with a loud "Nooooobody!"

Now that you've read the above encomium, your job is to answer the following questions as a means of analysis.[28]

1. What is the rhetorical situation that gave rise to this encomium?

2. Who is the author/speaker and does the author/speaker have any credibility to make the claims in the encomium?

3. Is the author intending to praise/defend or blame/attack that which is being spoken of?

4. Who is the author's intended audience?

5. Does the author succeed in conveying the intended message via an encomium (or mock-encomium)?

---

[28] These sample questions are loosely based on those taken from the Silva Rhetoricae website. I accessed the page with these and other questions on 2/12/18 at http://rhetoric.byu.edu/Pedagogy/Rhetorical%20Analysis%20heuristic.htm.

(12.2) Encomium & Invective

In this lesson, your charge is easy: write a mock encomium. Use the previously mentioned outline (also provided below but without the detailed specifics) in the construction of your encomium. You can choose from one of two topics: a sports team or someone famous.

Exordium
Origin
Nurture and Training
Accomplishments
Comparison
Noble Death and Posthumous Honors
Epilogue

[Use the blank space below and/or additional paper for composing.]

(12.3) Encomium & Invective

Here your goal is to compose a true encomium. Forget the sarcasm, as fun as it may be, and don't venture into invective land. Focus instead on either a) an individual who has figured prominently in your life, b) an animal that is and/or has been meaningful to you, or c) a specific place that is near and dear to you heart. Again, use the same outline.

Exordium
Origin
Nurture and Training
Accomplishments
Comparison
Noble Death and Posthumous Honors
Epilogue

[Use the blank space below and/or additional paper for composing.]

(12.4) Encomium & Invective

In this lesson your aim is to write an invective. As such, you're going to attack and blame someone or something. So as not to get too personal with anyone, your job is to write a vituperation of a well-known cartoon character. It can be a character from a movie, a television show, or a book/comic book. Use the same format for the invective as was used for the encomium.

Exordium
Origin
Nurture and Training
Accomplishments
Comparison
Noble Death and Posthumous Honors
Epilogue

[Use the blank space below and/or additional paper for composing.]

(12.5) Encomium & Invective

Throughout history, there have been various encomia and invectives that have assumed a poetic form. Writing in that tradition, your goal here is to create one or the other in a poetic form. These need not be terribly lengthy but you are asked to follow the same outline/format. Your composition topic can be either a) a favorite or most disliked food, or b) a favorite or most disliked weather phenomenon.

Exordium
Origin
Nurture and Training
Accomplishments
Comparison
Noble Death and Posthumous Honors
Epilogue

[Use the blank space below and/or additional paper for composing.]

(13.1) Description & Comparison

From my perspective, description and comparison are two of the easier elements of the progymnasmata to grasp. I think this is the case because they are likely among the most common and familiar. It is easy, for instance, to identify a descriptive piece from a non-descriptive one—the latter, of course, using more descriptors and precise terminology. Likewise, it's quite easy to spot a comparison or, in negative terms, a contrast. Comparisons/contrasts are in use in the everyday speech of most people.

Thus, these two items do not need much in the way of introductions. I do, however, like the definition of comparison offered by Crowley and Hawhee, namely, that it is "a double encomium or an encomium paired with an invective."[29] (If you need to, stop for a moment and ask yourself why that is the case.) As for description, it is what it sounds like. To be sure, however, it is not merely or simply the piling on of adjectives or participles to over-qualify something or someone.

To be descriptive in the purest sense means to be precise. As Marilyn McEntyre notes, "Precision is, after all, not only a form of responsibility and a kind of pleasure, but an instrument of compassion. To be precise requires care, time, and attention to the person, place, or process of being described."[30] Or, to put it more descriptively, perhaps, "Precise language surprises like a dancer's extra second of stillness in mid-air; word and experience come together in an irreproducible moment of epiphanic delight."[31]

Let us, then, engage one type of each writing in this chapter and ask some questions of each. The first, in line with description, is an excerpt from a work of long-time radio show host and celebrated author, Garrison Keillor. It is titled "Truckstop." The second, in line

---

[29] Sharon Crowley and Debra Hawhee, *Ancient Rhetorics for Contemporary Students* (New York: Pearson Longman, 2004), 407-08.

[30] Marilyn C. McEntyre, *Caring for Words in a Culture of Lies* (Grand Rapids: Eerdmans, 2009), 51.

[31] Ibid., 55.

with comparison, is from one of Shakespeare's most famous poems, Sonnet 18.

Truckstop

It has been a quiet week in Lake Wobegon. Florian and Myrtle Krebsbach left for Minneapolis on Tuesday, a long haul for them. They're no spring chickens, and it was cold and raining, and he hates to drive anyway. His eyesight is poor and his '66 Chev only has 47,000 miles on her, just like new, and he's proud of it. But Myrtle had to go down for a checkup. She can't get one from Dr. DeHaven or the doctors in Saint Cloud because she's had checkups from them recently and they say she is all right. She is pretty sure she might have cancer. She reads "Questions and Answers on Cancer" in the paper and has seen symptoms there that sound familiar, so when she found a lump on the back of her head last week and noticed blood on her toothbrush, she called a clinic in Minneapolis, made an appointment and off they went. He put on his good carcoat and a clean Pioneer Seed Corn cap, Myrtle wore a red dress so she would be safe in Minneapolis traffic. He got on Interstate 94 in Avon and headed south at forty miles an hour, hugging the right side, her clutching her purse, peering out of her thick glasses, semis blasting past them, both of them upset and scared, her about brain tumors, him about semis.[32]

1. Point out two instances where description is at work in the preceding piece. Are they precise or not?

---

[32] Garrison Keillor, "Truckstop," in *Leaving Home* (Place of publication not identified: Penguin Books, 1997), 60-61.

2. What led you to identify these two examples as description?

3. In an attempt to remain in keeping with the feel and style of this short excerpt, compose two sentences to tack on to the end.

Now that we have interacted with an example of description, let's turn our attention to comparison. It is important to note that comparison and contrast are often difficult to differentiate between. Don't get hung up on that, however, for if you've identified one or the other then you might as well treat them similarly. After you've read the poem below, answer the questions to help analyze it.

Sonnet 18

Shall I compare thee to a summer's day?
Thou art more lovely and more temperate:
Rough winds do shake the darling buds of May,
And summer's lease hath all too short a date:
Sometime too hot the eye of heaven shines,
And often is his gold complexion dimmed;
And every fair from fair sometime declines,
By chance, or nature's changing course, untrimmed:
But thy eternal summer shall not fade,
Nor lose possession of that fair thou ow'st,
Nor shall death brag thou wander'st in his shade
When in eternal lines to time thou grow'st:
So long as men can breathe or eyes can see,
So long lives this, and this gives life to thee.[33]

---

[33] William Shakespeare, *Shakespeare's Sonnets*, ed. K. Duncan-Jones (New York: Bloomsbury, 2016), 147.

1. In this poem, find one example of comparison and one of contrast. With what are they compared and contrasted?

2. What is the author's intended purpose and how does comparison/contrast help or hinder that?

3. Just below, compose four lines in the style of Shakespeare that you might add to this sonnet. You may add them in the beginning, middle, or end. Be sure you utilize comparison or contrast or both.

(13.2) Description & Comparison

In the brief excerpts throughout the remainder of this lesson, strive to pinpoint where description is present. If you identify examples, jot down a note or two about how they seem to be working or functioning in context. You are to do this in lieu of answering questions. The first excerpt comes from a short story by Flannery O'Connor titled "A View of the Woods." The second comes from the novel *Jayber Crow*, written by Kentucky native, Wendell Berry. The title of the chapter from which this is taken is "Goforth." Finally, another portion of text is taken from Jewish author, Chaim Potok, from the opening chapter of his volume *The Gift of Asher Lev*.

A View of the Woods

The week before, Mary Fortune and the old man had spent every morning watching the machine that lifted out dirt and threw it in a pile. The construction was going on by the new lakeside on one of the lots that the old man had sold to somebody who was going to put up a fishing club. He and Mary Fortune drove down there every morning about ten o'clock and he parked his car, a battered mulberry-colored Cadillac, on the embankment that overlooked the spot where the work was going on. The red corrugated lake eased up to within fifty feet of the construction and was bordered on the other side by a black line of woods which appeared at both ends of the view to walk across the water and continue along the edge of the fields. He sat on the bumper and Mary Fortune straddled the hood and they watched, sometimes for hours, while the machine systematically ate a square red hole in what had once been a cow pasture. It happened to be the only pasture that Pitts had succeeded in getting the bitterweed off and when the old man had sold it, Pitts had nearly had a stroke; and as far as Mr. Fortune was concerned, he could have gone on and had it.[34]

Thoughts/Comments:

"Goforth"

If you have lived in Port William a little more than two years, you are still, by Port William standards, a stranger, liable to have your name mispronounced. Crow was not a familiar name in this part of the country, and so for a long time a lot of people here called me Cray, a name that was familiar. And though I was only twenty-two when I came to the town, many of the same ones would call me "Mr. Cray" to acknowledge that they did not know me well. My rightful first name is Jonah, but I had not gone by that name since I was ten years old. I had been called simply J., and that was the way I signed myself. Once my customers took me to themselves, they called me Jaybird, and then Jayber. Thus I became, and have remained, a possession of Port William.

I was, in fact, a native as well as a newcomer, for I was born at Goforth, over on Katy's Branch, on August 3, 1914—and so lived one day in the world before the beginning of total war. You could say that Goforth was somewhat farther from Port William then than it is now; all that connected them then was a wagon road, imperfectly rocked, wondrously crooked, and bedeviled by mud holes. Goforth had its own church and school and store, but people

---

[34] Flannery O'Connor, "A View of the Woods," in *Everything that Rises Must Converge* (New York: Farrar, Straus and Giroux, 1993), 54-55.

from over there came to Port William to bank and vote and buy the things they could not buy at Goforth.[35]

Thoughts/Comments:

The Gift of Asher Lev

The taxi arrived. It was a lovely spring morning, the sun glistening on the red-pantiled houses of the villages, the air cool and clear and honey-colored all through the cypress-studded valley to the green hills and the sea. The driver helped me load the bags. I locked the house and the gate and we drove to Nice to the airport.

We were on line waiting to board the flight when Avrumel, five years old and still confused by the abrupt wrenching from his comfortable world, suddenly realized he had forgotten to bring Shimson, the Samson rag doll that had been his companion since birth and with which he held long, intimate conversations. He began to cry. Devorah said she was sure we would be able to buy him a new Shimson doll in New York, but he was inconsolable. She held him as he cried. Eleven-year-old Rocheleh, pale of face and large of eyes, said, in her tone of grownup disdain, "He's such a child."

Avrumel had on his high red sneakers and green jogging suit. He sat next to me in the airbus, weeping. I took my drawing pad and a soft-leaded pencil from my attaché case and quickly drew from memory an exact and realistic picture of Shimshon, shading it into three-dimensionality with the side of my small finger. Avrumel watched through his tears as his rag doll came to life under the point of my pencil: frayed right ear, gouged right eye, thick-chested, broad-shouldered, wearing a tunic and sandals, its chiseled face

---

[35] Wendell Berry, "Goforth," in *Jayber Crow: A Novel* (Washington, D.C.: Crosspoint, 2000), 11-12.

topped by an enormous shock of hair. I gave him the drawing, and his freckled face broke into a smile of delight.[36]

Thoughts/Comments:

---

[36] Chaim Potok, *The Gift of Asher Lev* (New York: Fawcett Books, 1997), 4-5.

(13.3) Description & Comparison

In this lesson the focus is on comparison and contrast. As in the previous lesson, when you identify examples, jot down a few notes about how they seem to be working or functioning in context. You are to do this in lieu of answering questions. The first excerpt comes from *Night*, a book by Elie Wiesel, a Nobel Peace Prize winner and Jewish author who survived the Holocaust. The second bit comes from *Strange Case of Dr. Jekyll and Mr. Hyde*, written by Robert Louis Stevenson.

Night

By day I studied Talmud and by night I would run to the synagogue to weep over the destruction of the Temple. One day I asked my father to find me a master who could guide me in my studies of Kabbalah...My father was a cultured man, rather unsentimental. He rarely displayed his feelings, not even within his family, and was more involved with the welfare of others than with that of his own kin...He wanted to drive the idea of studying Kabbalah from my mind. In vain. I succeeded on my own in finding a master for myself in the person of Moishe the Beadle.

He had watched me one day as I prayed at dusk. "Why do you cry when you pray?" he asked, as though he knew me well. "I don't know," I answered, troubled. I had never asked myself that question. I cried because ... because something inside me felt the need to cry. That was all I knew. "Why do you pray?" he asked after a moment. Why did I pray? Strange question. Why did I live? Why did I breathe?

"I don't know," I told him, even more troubled and ill at ease. "I don't know." From that day on, I saw him often. He explained to me, with great emphasis, that every question possessed a power that was lost in the answer. Man comes closer to God through the questions he asks Him, he liked to say...We spoke that way almost every evening, remaining in the synagogue long after all

the faithful had gone, sitting in the semidarkness where only a few half-burnt candles provided a flickering light...And Moishe the Beadle, the poorest of the poor of Sighet, spoke to me for hours on end about the Kabbalah's revelations and its mysteries. Thus began my initiation. Together we would read, over and over again, the same page of Zohar. Not to learn it by heart but to discover within the very essence of divinity...And then, one day all foreign Jews were expelled from Sighet. And Moishe the Beadle was a foreigner.

Crammed into cattle cars by the Hungarian police, they cried silently. Standing on the station platform, we too were crying. The train disappeared over the horizon; all that was left was thick, dirty smoke. The deportees were quickly forgotten...Days went by. Then weeks and months. Life was normal again. A calm, reassuring wind blew through our homes. The shopkeepers were doing good business, the students lived among their books, and the children played in the streets.

One day, as I was about to enter the synagogue, I saw Moishe the Beadle sitting on a bench near the entrance. He told me what had happened to him and his companions. The train with the deportees had crossed the Hungarian border and, once in Polish territory, had been taken over by the Gestapo. The train had stopped. The Jews were ordered to get off and onto waiting trucks. The trucks headed toward a forest. There everybody was ordered to get out. They were forced to dig huge trenches. When they had finished their work, the men from the Gestapo began theirs. Without passion or haste, they shot the prisoners, who were forced to approach the trench one by one and offer their necks. Infants were tossed into the air and used as targets for the machine guns. This took place in the Galician forest, near Kolomay. How had he, Moishe the Beadle, been able to escape. By a miracle. He was wounded in the leg and left for dead.

Day after day, night after night, he went from one Jewish house to the next, telling his story and that of Malka, the young girl who lay dying for three days, and that of Tobie, the tailor who begged to die before his sons were killed. Moishe was not the same.

The joy in his eyes was gone. He no longer sang. He no longer mentioned either God or Kabbalah. He spoke only of what he had seen. But people not only refused to believe his tales, they refused to listen. Some even insinuated that he only wanted their pity, that he was imagining things. Others flatly said that he had gone mad.

As for Moishe, he wept and pleaded: "Jews, listen to me! That's all I ask of you. No money. No pity. Just listen to me!" he kept shouting in the synagogue, between the prayer at dusk and the evening prayer. Even I did not believe him. I often sat with him, after services, and listened to his tales, trying to understand his grief. But all I felt was pity.[37]

Thoughts/Comments:

Strange Case of Dr. Jekyll and Mr. Hyde

Mr. Utterson the lawyer was a man of a rugged countenance, that was never lighted by a smile; cold, scanty and embarrassed in discourse; backward in sentiment; lean, long, dusty, dreary and yet somehow loveable...But he had an approved tolerance for others; sometimes wondering, almost with envy, at the high pressure of spirits involved in their misdeeds; and in any extremity inclined to help rather than to reprove...he never marked a shade of change in his demeanor.

No doubt the feat was easy to Mr. Utterson; for he was undemonstrative at the best, and even his friendships seemed to be founded in a similar catholicity of good-nature. It is the mark of a modest man to accept his friendly circle ready-made from the hands of opportunity; and that was the lawyer's way. His friends were those of his own blood or those whom he had known the longest; his

---

[37] Elie M. Wiesel, *Night* (New York: Hill and Wang, 2006), 4-7.

affections, like ivy, were the growth of time, they implied no aptness in the object. Hence, no doubt, the bond that united him to Mr. Richard Enfield, his distant kinsman, the well-known man about town. It was a nut to crack for many, what these two could see in each other, or what subject they could find in common. It was reported by those who encountered them in their Sunday walks, that they said nothing, looked singularly dull, and would hail with obvious relief the appearance of a friend. For all that, the two men put the greatest store by these excursions, counted them the chief jewel of each week, and not only set aside occasions of pleasure, but even resisted the calls of business, that they might enjoy them uninterrupted.

It chanced on one of these rambles that their way led them down a by-street in a busy quarter of London. The street was small and what is called quiet, but it drove a thriving trade on weekdays. The inhabitants were all doing well, it seemed, and all emulously hoping to do better still, and layout out the surplus of their gains in coquetry; so that the shop fronts stood along that thoroughfare with an air of invitation, like rows of smiling saleswomen. Even on Sunday, when it veiled its more florid charms and lay comparatively empty of passage, the street shone out in contrast to its dingy neighborhood, like a fire in a forest; and with its freshly painted shutters, well polished brasses, and general cleanliness and gaiety of note, instantly caught and pleased the eye of the passenger.[38]

Thoughts/Comments:

---

[38] Robert Louis Stevenson, *Strange Case of Dr. Jekyll and Mr. Hyde* (New York: Scriber's Sons, 1886), 2-4.

(13.4) Description & Comparison

In Lesson 13.4 your task is to choose one of the excerpts in 13.2 and attempt to write two or three paragraphs that either precede it, fall within the middle of it, or come after it. One of your goals is to attempt to maintain the tone and feel of the piece. You will do that through the language you choose to use. Your original paragraphs should read seamlessly with the writing you are adding to. Others, then, should not be able to tell which portion is yours and which is the original author's. Use the remainder of this page and, perhaps, the next, to compose. Or, use a separate sheet of paper.

[Use the blank space below and/or additional paper for composing.]

(13.5) Description & Comparison

In the preceding lesson you choose a descriptive piece to add to. Here, you will do much the same, except you need to use one of the comparative or contrastive bits from 13.3. Once again, you may add your two or three original paragraphs to the beginning, middle, or end. In fact, you might even want to add a paragraph at each of those three locations. Whatever you choose, strive to give the piece a seamless feel. Use the remainder of this page and, perhaps, the next, to compose. Or, use a separate sheet of paper.

[Use the blank space below and/or additional paper for composing.]

(14.1) Impersonation

In the ancient world the concept of imitation was prevalent among teachers of speech and writing. It was displayed in *mimesis* and *imitatio*. The former was often related to imitating people or things while the latter usually had to do with writing and literature.[39] Even so, there was often considerable overlap between these and related terms and their meanings.

With regard to rhetoric and composition, teachers often taught their students via imitation. That is, they would often show their disciples examples and then have them copy those selections word for word, compose original phrases or clauses using similar grammatical and syntactical features, adopt similar terminology, paraphrase, summarize, and more. With that tradition in mind, in this lesson, which is a bit longer than usual, as well as the next several lessons, you will practice the art of imitation. The hope is that these activities will help sharpen your skills as a writer and rhetor.

Here in 14.1 we will start with the imitation of phrases and then move to clauses and sentences. All of the examples are taken from sentences found in Annie Dillard's novel *Pilgrim at Tinker Creek*.[40] The first type of phrase to consider is a noun phrase. A noun phrase can consist of a noun standing by itself or with some sort of modifier, such as a definite article. Below are several noun phrases that go from less to more sophisticated. Your job is to imitate these phrases and come up with ones on your own. Write them in the empty column below.

Window	
The window	

---

[39] For a further discussion of this, see the "Introduction" by Jonathan Holmes and Adrian Streete in *Refiguring Mimesis: Representation in Early Modern Literature*, eds. J. Holmes and A. Streete (Hertfordshire: University of Hertfordshire Press, 2005), 1-11.

[40] Annie Dillard, *Pilgrim at Tinker Creek* (San Francisco: HarperCollins e-books, 2007).

The open window	

Another type of phrase is the prepositional phrase. This is a phrase that functions as a modifier and begins with a preposition. In addition, it will contain at least one other substantive (i.e. a word or string of words functioning as a noun) that follows. This substantive is referred to by grammarians as the "object of the preposition." Once again, imitate the composition below by creating something original yet similar.

Before	
Before the mirror	
In	
In a daze	
Before the mirror in a daze	

If you were paying attention, you might have noticed that the two preceding prepositional phrases had noun phrases embedded in them. The noun phrases are "mirror" and "the mirror" as well as "daze" and "a daze." There are many other types of phrases: verb phrases, participial phrases, gerund phrases, infinitive phrases, restrictive and non-restrictive phrases, etc. A verb phrase is a phrase functioning as a verb and often contains a helping word. Create some of your own examples like those below.

Used to have	
Could have been	

Another common part of speech is the participle. Simply put, a participle is a verbal adjective—the dictionary form of a verb with -ing or -ed added to the end. As a verbal adjective, participles are able to function like adjectives and qualify or modify other parts of speech, such as nouns and adjectives. Imitate the following forms and create your own.

fighting	
fighting tom	
graveled	
graveled shallows	

The next type of example is a gerund phrase. Gerunds are similar to participles in that they have an -ing ending and are built on verbs. The main difference between the two, however, is that while a participle is a verbal adjective, a gerund is a verbal noun. Put differently, while a participle functions as an adjective that modifies or qualifies a noun, a gerund actually functions as the noun itself. Thus, a participle can modify a gerund as in "this boring studying." Imitate the gerunds and gerund phrases below and create your own.

imagining	
imagining the yard	

Also common in speech and composition are infinitives. An infinitive is often described as the lexical form of a verb. Thus, "dance," "cook," and "run" are all words you would find as dictionary entries. These become infinitive phrases when you add "to" to them. Thus, "to run," "to cook," and "to sing" are all infinitive phrases. Using the examples, create your own infinitive phrases.

find	
to find	
explore	
to explore	

Now that we have focused on and created examples at the phrase level, let's turn our attention to clauses. The main difference between a phrase and a clause is that the latter has both a subject and a predicate while the former does not. It should be noted, however, that simply because a clause contains both a subject and a predicate, it does not mean that it is or has to be complete. If a clause can stand alone as a complete sentence, we can actually call it a complete sentence. If, however, a clause cannot stand alone as a complete sentence, it, of course, cannot be deemed a complete sentence.

There are two very common terms that function as synonyms, which are used to describe a stand-alone clause: "independent" and "main." Although these types of clauses can stand by themselves, they often connect with other clauses. In fact, they can connect with other independent clauses. Likewise, they can connect with clauses that cannot stand alone—clauses that depend on them to complete the meaning. Such clauses are known synonymously as "dependent" or "subordinate." In the first set of boxes below, you will find some independent clauses that you should imitate. Write your sentences in the blank boxes beneath each typed entry. In the second set of boxes, you will find some dependent clauses with which you should do the same.

I washed before the mirror in a daze,
My twisted summer sleep still hung about me like sea kelp.
I washed before the mirror in a daze, my twisted summer sleep still hung about me like sea kelp.

In the examples above, notice that there are two independent clauses. And note, too, that simply by virtue of adding a comma, we joined them together. Unfortunately, if you were to show this to most grammar teachers, they would cringe. Why? Because this is supposedly "against the rules." It results in what is known as a comma splice.

The so-called correct way to join together two independent clauses is either by a) Placing a period or semicolon between the two clauses, b) Placing a comma at the end of the first clause and a coordinating conjunction right after it, c) Placing a semicolon at the end of the first clause and a conjunctive adverb right after it, or d) Changing one of the clauses into a dependent clause. While I affirm these solutions, I also hold the view that a comma splice isn't necessarily and always an error.

On the contrary: a comma splice can be used to achieve a certain type of style and affect. The comma splice, as in Dillard's sentence above, demonstrates to me that the thoughts are overlapping. Thus, this can be used strategically when an author wants to convey something simultaneous that rather than including a period, comma, or semicolon that might seem to indicate a break or distinction. To see what I am alluding to, contrast the sentence above with the one below where two independent clauses are connected by a comma immediately followed by a conjunction.

Today is one of those excellent January partly cloudies in which light chooses an unexpected part of the landscape to trick out in gilt,
And then shadow sweeps it away.
Today is one of those excellent January partly cloudies in which light chooses an unexpected part of the landscape to trick out in gilt, and then shadow sweeps it away.

Did you contrast the sentences? See! The comma splice works effectively to show the overlap of looking at one's tired self in the mirror while washing. The comma and conjunction, however, work to show separation—the light peeking through and subsequently being swept away by the darkness of a shadow. So, I affirm the use of a comma splice but only when it is used well and with the intent of showing overlapping thoughts, ideas, etc. Having said that, here are a couple more examples to imitate various ways to avoid splicing.

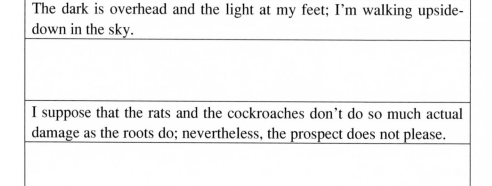

The next type of clause to consider is the adverb clause. This is also known as an oblique clause or, more commonly, a subordinate (conjunctive) clause. Adverb clauses are also referred to as subordinate conjunctive clauses because, although they begin with conjunctions, grammatically speaking, the clauses actually function like adverbs and, thus, typically modify verbs or verb phrases. Consider the examples below and imitate them. Note how they appear at different locations within each of the sentences.

| We wake, [if we ever wake at all], to mystery, rumors of death, beauty, violence.... |
| |
| One patient called lemonade "square" [because it pricked on his tongue as a square shape pricked on the touch of his hands]. |
| |
| [If things aren't altered], I'll tear my eyes out. |
| |

Another type of clause is the adjective clause. This is also known as the relative clause. These types of clauses do not start with adjectives; rather, they begin with relative pronouns or relative adverbs. For example, relative clauses might have terms like *who*, *which*, and *that*, all relative pronouns, at the start. Some relative adverbs you may find are terms like *when* or *where*. These are referred to as adjective clauses because they modify the nominal that precedes. Below, look at some of the examples and then create your own that are similar.

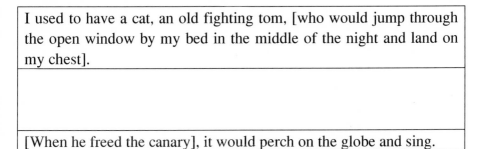

I used to have a cat, an old fighting tom, [who would jump through the open window by my bed in the middle of the night and land on my chest].
[When he freed the canary], it would perch on the globe and sing.

Up next for consideration is the elliptical clause. Ellipsis is a grammatical term that means to remove or drop out—to elide. Thus, in an elliptical clause, a word drops out and, thus, is missing. Well, it is missing in print at least. I say "at least" because in an elliptical clause the missing word is implied. Native speakers of a language like English inherently and immediately know which words are missing and implied but rarely ever think about them—it's simply understood. In the next set of boxes, consider a couple of examples and then create your own in a similar fashion.

These are morning matters, pictures [that] you dream as the final wave heaves you up on the sand to the bright light and drying air.

I had read about the giant water bug, but [I had] never seen one.

Now, let's consider restrictive and non-restrictive clauses. The former is a type of clause whose intent is to restrict or limit meaning. Stated differently, a restrictive clause specifies exactly which noun it is modifying by way of process of elimination. In the example below, which you should imitate, notice that the bracketed clause is limited to modifying only one noun, the only one that it could possibly be referring to (i.e. wolf). It is not referring to other nouns like "sense" or "God" or "house" or "turkey" that appear in the sentence.

Was the sense of it there, and God absconded with it, ate it, like a wolf [who disappears round the edge of the house with the Thanksgiving turkey]?

A nonrestrictive clause does not limit like a restrictive clause does. To be sure, it still functions as a modifier and adds additional, but not wholly necessary, information to the sentence. Its job, however, is not to narrow down the possibilities of which noun it might be referring to. As a result and as a means of helping readers figure that out, a nonrestrictive clause, also known as an appositive clause, because it has no limiting effect, has a comma on both sides of it. Once again, look at the following example and then create your own, which should be similar.

He was exactly half in and half out of the water[, looking like a schematic diagram of an amphibian,] and he didn't jump.

The final type of clause to consider and imitate here is the complement clause. Note first that the term "complement" is not the same as "compliment." Our use of "complement" is similar in meaning to the word "complete." Thus, complement clauses are clauses that help complete the idea of a sentence. Complement clauses, at least as we're going to describe them here, typically function as one entire subject or object of another clause. In some sense, then, when one uses a complement clause, they are embedding one clause in another. The use of a complement clause shows a certain level of sophistication in speaking or writing. Look at the examples below and imitate them.

[That it's rough out there and chancy] is no surprise.

Galileo thought [comets were an optical illusion].

(14.2) Impersonation

In Lesson 14.2 the goal is to consider a number of different sentence types and structures and then imitate them. Now that you have numerous types of phrases and clauses readily available and at your disposal, the activities here should be quite easy. As with the previous lesson, I will be excerpting examples from Annie Dillard's novel titled *Pilgrim at Tinker Creek*.

The first type of sentence to consider is the declarative sentence. A declarative sentence is a sentence that declares something, it makes a statement about something. As such, these types of sentences have a period after them. Below are a couple of sentences worthy of consideration and imitation. In your imitation, strive to use the same parts of speech and word order of phrases and clauses to create an original sentence.

The sign on my body could have been an emblem or a stain, the keys to the kingdom or the mark of Cain.
You can heave your spirit into a mountain and the mountain will keep it, folded, and not throw it back as some creeks will.

The next type of sentence to consider is the imperative sentence. This kind of sentence issues a command. As such, it usually orders someone to do something. Imperatives sometimes have a period at the end and sometimes an exclamation point. Use the following examples and, once again, imitate them to the best of your ability. Work hard to employ similar syntactical devices and follow word order.

> Suggested emendation in the Lord's Prayer: Take out 'Thy Kingdom come' and substitute 'Give us time!'
>
>
>
> Pull yourself together.
>
>

The third type of sentence to consider is the interrogative. This type has to do with asking questions. Just think—as the word implies—of interrogation. Think of a cold dark room where cross-examinations by detectives occur. What do they do there? They interrogate! They ask questions of those in the hot seat. Read the sentences below and imitate them.

> What prevents the men on Palomar from falling, voiceless and blinded, from their tiny, vaulted chairs?
>
>
>
> What did the girl think of her father's dragging her lover all over town by the hair?
>
>

Another kind of sentence is the exclamatory sentence. This term, too, as the name implies, it exclaims something. As such, the typical punctuation mark at the end of this type of sentence is—Surprise! Surprise!—an exclamation point. (See what I did there?!) And do you see what I did in the statement in parentheses, too? In modern writing it has become very common to see question marks and exclamation marks paired together when an interrogative sentence also functions in a way that gives it the sense of an exclamation. This often happens with rhetorical questions.

While Annie Dillard does not actually do this in her novel, she does use an interrogative as an exclamation but only puts the exclamation mark at the end. It is the last of the three examples below. But note, too, the second example. There the exclamatory remark is actually not a complete sentence; rather, it is an exclamatory statement. That is very common, too. With these things in mind, use the examples below to create your own original exclamatory sentences.

Lightning! Copperhead! Swedish meatballs!
That a live creature spends thirteen consecutive years scrabbling around in the root systems of trees in the dark and damp—thirteen years!—is amply boggling for me.
What could I not do if I had the power and will of a mole!

The fifth type of sentence under consideration is a simple sentence. This type of sentence contains a subject and a predicate. A subject is who or what the sentence brings into focus and, stated simply, a predicate is what is said about that which has been brought into focus (i.e. the subject). In the examples below, draw a circle around the subject, underline the predicate (i.e. everything else), and then create similar sentences.

I visited an aunt and uncle at a quarter-horse ranch in Cody, Wyoming.

I used to be able to see flying insects in the air.

Next up for review is the compound sentence. A compound sentence is formed when two independent clauses are joined together. As you saw in the previous lesson, one way to do this is with a comma-conjunction pair. This can also be done with a semicolon or, if you know how to do it well, with a comma splice. Really, you can think of compound sentences like compound words. In compound words two (or more) words are melded together to make one. In a compound sentence, two independent clauses, that is, two complete sentences, are joined together to make one. Some examples have been given below to imitate. Note, in particular, the second one, which has three independent clauses and uses two ways of connecting them to make a compound.

It is winter proper; the cold weather, such as it is, has come to stay.

At night I read and write, and things I have never understood become clear; I reap the harvest of the rest of the year's planting.

Now it is time to give attention to complex sentences. This genre of sentence, which should already be somewhat familiar to you, consists of one independent clause that is joined to one or more dependent/subordinate clauses. The quick way to identify these is to look for subordinating conjunctions or conjunctive adverbs like *that*, *who*, or *which*. As usual, there are a couple examples below to consider and imitate.

Although there are engineers at the throttles, no one is manning the switches.

Monarchs have always been assumed to taste terribly bitter, because of the acrid milkweed on which the caterpillars feed.

The final type of sentence to consider here is the compound complex sentence. As you might have intuited, this is a combination of a compound sentence and a complex sentence. What this means is that the resultant sentence will have at least two independent clauses and one or more dependent clauses. Look at the sentences below and, after attempting to identify each clause, imitate them by creating your own.

After the one extravagant gesture of creation in the first place, the universe has continued to deal exclusively in extravagances, flinging intricacies and colossi down aeons of emptiness, heaping profusions on profligacies with ever-fresh vigor.

After the silt settles I return and see tracings of minute snails on the bottom, a planarian or two winding round the rim of water, roundworms shimmying frantically, and finally, when my eyes have adjusted to these dimensions, amoebae.

(14.3) Impersonation

Now that you have imitated phrases, clauses, and sentences, we're going to graduate up to paragraphs. As in the previous two lessons, I am going to use the work of Annie Dillard as an example for you to imitate. Why? Because she is a great writer and someone worth emulating. Below are two paragraphs. Your task is to follow the word order of each sentence in the creation of your own unique paragraph. Your paragraph can be about whatever you want it to be about. The important thing here is to try as hard as possible to follow Dillard's word order and use of syntactical and rhetorical devices. Use the remaining space below and the space on the next page to compose.

When I was quite young I fondly imagined that all foreign languages were codes for English. I thought that "hat," say, was the real and actual name of the thing, but that people in other countries, who obstinately persisted in speaking the code of their forefathers, might use the word "ibu," say, to designate not merely the concept hat, but the English word "hat." I knew only one foreign word, "oui," and since it had three letters as did the word for which it was a code, it seemed, touchingly enough, to confirm my theory. Each foreign language was a different code, I figured, and at school I would eventually be given the keys to unlock some of the most important codes' systems. Of course I knew that it might take years before I became so fluent in another language that I could code and decode easily in my head, and make of gibberish a nimble sense. On the first day of my first French course, however, things rapidly took on an entirely unexpected shape. I realized that I was going to have to learn speech all over again, word by word, one word at a time—and my dismay knew no bounds.

[Use the blank space below and/or additional paper for composing.]

Here is another paragraph from Dillard to imitate. Again, use the remaining space below and on the next page to compose.

It's summer. We had some deep spring sunshine about a month ago, in a drought; the nights were cold. It's been gray sporadically, but not oppressively, and rainy for a week, and I would think: When is the real hot stuff coming, the mind-melting weeding weather? It was rainy again this morning, the same spring rain, and then this afternoon a different rain came: a pounding, three-minute shower. And when it was over, the cloud dissolved to haze. I can't see Tinker Mountain. It's summer now: the heat is on. It's summer now all summer long.

[Use the blank space below and/or additional paper for composing.]

(14.4) Impersonation

Moving up from composing just a paragraph, your task now is to write a very short story. While you are to create your own original work, your goal is to try to closely imitate the story below— my translation of the parable of "The Good Samaritan" (Lk 10:30-37), taken from the New Testament. Try to use similar sentence devices as well as sentence and paragraph structures when composing.

Jesus said: "A certain man was going down from Jerusalem into Jericho and he fell among bandits who, both after stripping him and putting gashes upon him, departed, leaving him half-dead. Well, by chance, a certain priest was going down on that road and, having seen him, passed on the opposite side. Similarly, however, a Levite also happened upon the place and, after coming and seeing, passed on the opposite side."

"So, a certain Samaritan came upon him and, after seeing, was compassionate. And after he approached, he wrapped up his wounds, while pouring on oil and wine. Moreover, after he sat him upon his own animal, he brought him to an inn and took care of him. And on the next day, having taken out two coins, he gave them to the innkeeper and said, 'Take care of him, and whatever certain amount that you might spend, I, on returning, will repay you.'"

(Jesus said:) "Which of these three, seems to have been a neighbor to the one fallen among the bandits?"

Well, the (lawyer) said: "The one having done mercy to him."

Jesus said to him, "So, go and you yourself do similarly!"

[Use the blank space below and/or additional paper for composing.]

(14.5) Impersonation

Lesson 14.5 is your last on impersonation or imitation. Once again, your task is to emulate the writing below. This particular entry comes from the journal of one of my forefathers in the Christian faith, John Wesley. He penned this in his journal in 1736 while traveling by boat across the sea. Read this and, once again, imitate it. This time, in addition to imitating the sentence and paragraph elements, also imitate the genre and archaic language. Use the white space below and/or an additional sheet of paper.

(Friday, January 23, 1736) In the evening another storm began. In the morning it increased, so that they were forced to let the ship drive. I could not but say to myself, "How is it that thou hast no faith?" being still unwilling to die. About one in the afternoon, almost as soon as I had stepped out of the great cabin door, the sea did not break as usual, but came with a full, smooth tide over the side of the ship. I was vaulted over with water in a moment, and so stunned that I scarce expected to lift up my head again, till the sea should give up her dead. But thanks be to God, I received no hurt at all. About midnight the storm ceased.

(15.1) Thesis & Law

Since "law" will be introduced in Lesson 15.3, in both 15.1 and 15.2, "thesis" is the focus. The term "thesis," which is well known by many English speakers, comes from the ancient Greek term θέσις (pronounced: theh-cease). It was a word with an incredibly wide semantic range but, in terms of rhetoric and philosophy, it had a literal meaning of "to lay/put down" (related to the verb τίθημι, "I place/put," whose imperative form is θές, and from the Proto-Indo-European root *dhe, also meaning "to place, put, lay"). Thus, an orator engaging in the practice of thesis was laying down an argument. If one were to follow the lead of Aelius Theon, they would understand a thesis to have among it the following traits:

1. a verbal inquiry;
2. admits controversy;
3. typically, deals with a general matter unlike "hypothesis," which is often specific;
4. concerned with something in doubt;
5. end-result is to persuade;
6. delivered in an assembly or lecture hall;
7. spoken before citizens in general;
8. no narratio;
9. some being theoretical; and,
10. some being practical.[41]

The structure of a thesis may follow the six (or five, depending on how you define/describe them) Latin *partes orationis* (parts of speech): exordium, narratio, partitio, confirmatio, refutatio, and

---

[41] Kennedy, *Progymnasmata*, 55-56.

peroratio.[42] Yet, Theon, in description and practice, seems to opt for a different outline: subtle approach, first antithesis, first solution, second antithesis, second solution, third antithesis, third solution, and conclusion.[43] Personally, I believe the latter approach is the better one suited for this genre. William Weaver, in discussing this matter so well, is worth citing here:

> *So far, the student has been engaged in writing mocked-up speeches, solo enunciations of a theme, narrative, or argument. But now the student must respond as if in rebuttal—must even produce the arguments to which he responds. Of course, the spontaneity of **antithesis** is contrived, just as all of the progymnasmata are contrived. But it nonetheless represents a major cognitive step, a*

---

[42] The position I take on the structure of a thesis may be tempered by other views. See, for instance, the following quote, which is taken from Craig A. Gibson, *Libanius's* Progymnasmata: *Model Exercises in Greek Prose Composition and Rhetoric*, ed. M. Heath (WGW 27; Atlanta: Society of Biblical Literature), 509: "After a brief introduction, the exercise in thesis is elaborated according to the so-called 'final headings': just, advantageous, possible ([Hermogenes] 25–26; Aphthonius 42), legal (Aphthonius 42), and appropriate ([Hermogenes] 26). (A more extensive method of elaboration is found in Theon 121–122.) Nicolaus, on the other hand, recommends using the same headings as for encomium (72–74). A thesis should also include rebuttals of hypothetical objections (Aphthonius 42; Nicolaus 74–75), as the examples in this collection do (see Thesis 1.26, 2.6, 2.9, 3.5, 3.7)." Another view, asserted by Stuart Bryan and Jared Miller, is that "The parts of a thesis are simply the parts of a classical discourse" (55), namely, the exordium, narratio, partitio, confirmatio, refutatio, and peroratio. See their assertions in *Omnibus III: Reformation to the Present*, eds. D. Wilson and G.T. Fischer (Lancaster, PA: Veritas, 2006), 55 and 370. This is also stated by Robert J. Pnella, "The *Progmynmasmata* and Progynasmatic Theory in Imperial Greek Education," in *A Companion to Ancient Education*, ed. M. Bloomer (Malden, Mass.: John Wiley & Sons, 2015). Pnella, referencing Nicolaus, notes that, "Thesis also provides exercise in all five parts of the oration" (168). What these differences in structure seem to come down to is which rhetor one follows most closely (i.e. Theon, Aphthonius, Nicolaus, Libanius, Hermogones, etc.).

[43] Ibid., 121.

significant move from the formulas of the earlier themes to something like the extempore give and take of the assembly and law courts, the public venues undoubtedly mimicked in **thesis** *and* **legislation**.[44]

Another aspect of the thesis that Weaver both enunciates and clarifies, one which I really believe captures the essence of the thesis, is that it is meant to reclaim. Again, he is worth citing: "The discipline of *thesis* is not, then, just to refute the arguments of another—that we have seen in **confutatio** and **confirmatio**—but more importantly to reclaim the discourse from another voice, to respond without losing control over the terms of the controversy."[45] The one engaging in thesis, then, is engaging in a controversy and, if he or she does it well, they will reclaim and maintain control of the discourse while also bolstering their arguments with persuasive demeanor.

If the thesis is concerned with things general rather than specific, then the antithesis is concerned with specific things. The antithesis is the "second voice" that Weaver spoke about above. It is the voice of one's opponent(s); the voice of the speaker anticipating their refutations and debunking them ahead of time.

There were two main types of thesis: practical and theoretical. The former dealt with practical matters while the latter was concerned with more abstract and, as the name suggests, theoretical concerns. On some occasions, a thesis and an antithesis might be brought together to form a synthesis. That is, an orator might find a happy medium or middle ground, a good solution, so to speak, in synthesizing the two seemingly opposite arguments. This was a good strategy because, at one and the same time, it appeared that the orator was conceding some but, in the end, might succeed most in persuading his or her audience.

---

[44] William Weaver, *Untutored Lines: The Making of the English Epyllion* (Edinburgh: Edinburgh University Press, 2012), 181.

[45] Ibid. Here, "confutation" is functioning as a synonym for "refutatio."

With these items in mind, it is time to do a bit of analysis. Just below, in using Theon's tripartite thesis/antithesis approach, I have composed an original thesis. This, in fact, is the transcript of a TEDx Talk I gave in Evansville, Indiana, in 2015. It is an argument of the practical type in which I discuss the matter of attempting to revive or resurrect dead languages. So, read the thesis below, analyze it, and then answer the questions that follow.

Subtle Approach: What comes to mind when you hear the word endangered? Yeah, animals probably! The black rhino, the blue whale, green turtle, Yaghan, or Yarawi. Now, those last two that I just mentioned, as some of you may well know, actually aren't animals at all, they're languages. To be more particular, they're two of the most endangered languages in the world, surviving on something like the equivalent of linguistic life support; in fact, of the nearly 6,000 languages in use across the globe today, some estimate that about half of those are currently endangered. Now, thankfully, there are organizations, quite like those who are out to help save the whales, whose goal is to aid in preserving these endangered speech species.

Antithesis 1: But what if it's too late? What if a language has already been assigned its death certificate? What does one do, for example, with any of the nearly 600 languages that have already been declared dead?

Solution 1: Well, there's a growing contingent, a community of men and women across the continents, who may have some ideas worth spreading, ideas rooted in the soils of rebirth and renewal. These teachers and students and researchers alike are propelled by linguistic creativity and an insatiable drive to see and hear these tongues unfettered from the chains of the past.

Antithesis 2: But why?

Solution 2: Well, *en route* to answering those two questions, let me first offer a couple of admissions. So, first admission: Somewhere along the way, I bought into the lie, I subscribed to the myth, that I was bad at languages, that I was bad at learning languages. Now, I grew up in a context, in an environment where English was the norm. English was the only thing spoken and, so, exposure to other languages was practically non-existent—unless, of course, you count sleeping through French and Spanish classes in high school as exposure to other languages.

But even then, as a monolingual, whenever I heard those other languages spoken, I was blown away; I was fascinated. And that same fascination was present when I traveled to Israel for the first time a number of years ago and had what I might refer to as a "tipping point" experience—which leads me to my second admission. During my time there in Israel, I found myself day after day among a group of folks and we were attempting to resurrect a dead language mainly by speaking it.

No, not ancient Hebrew! In this case, Koine Greek, which is a version of Ancient Greek. And it was dawning on me like, "I'm capable. We're capable. We humans, we're wired to use and speak languages." And that's but one of the reasons why we might take a greater interest in resurrecting dead languages—because we can!

And here's another: We inhabit a world today where, believe it or not, on average one language may be passing away about every other week. So, resurrecting a dead language is not merely a means of recovering some history—although, it is that!—but it's also a means of reanimating some history. Just like there's beauty to be found in polishing and restoring artifacts or realia, languages are beautiful treasures of history that we can uniquely reawaken.

And here's a third reason: Even if the revitalization of a stilled or inert tongue is undertaken say, just because I want to know it, that is, out of my own interest, then that's still a perfectly worthwhile endeavor. Yes, there may be self-centered and or group-centered motives or ambitions behind that but, in all honesty, that's central to the vitality and survival of any language. Language transmission depends on these kinds of things.

And I could give numerous other reasons why, but I want to offer just one more: Ancient texts like the Bible. Now, there's no doubt that the Bible has played a big role in world history in general and it's no secret that the Bible has had a profound influence on American history and culture in particular. And that's precisely one of the reasons why handling such a prominent text requires extreme care. Being equipped to sufficiently interact with the Bible in the languages it was first written in, namely, ancient Hebrew, Aramaic, and Greek, can be very important.

Just like there's some other languages that we could interact with, by engaging the Hebrew, Aramaic, and Greek, we can help learners navigate those texts and we can find our way through the text. At the end of the day, the Bible is likely always going to be around and it's likely always going to be a talking point. And, so, we can't simply dismiss it and/or its adherents outright; instead, what's needed is a healthy, knowledgeable, and responsible engagement with it.

Antithesis 3: Well, those are some of the reasons "why," but what about the "how" question—how does one go about restoring the pulse to a stopped language?

Solution 3: Briefly, I want to offer just three suggestions—there are many more!—but these are drawn mainly from my own experience as one attempting to do this with the Conversational Koine Institute. An early step in resurrecting a dead language is to begin recovering native resources and, once we've done this, we can begin dredging or mining them for helpful data.

In my case, for example, because I like to work with ancient languages like those of the Bible, the natural place to begin is with ancient texts and these come in many different forms. Now, obviously I don't have the luxury of tapping into an audio or video recording made by say, some ancient Greek person, but, spending time with the deposit of texts available is an option and much can be learned about the language from this.

A subsequent step is to begin creating a community or communities where the language becomes a focal point. Everyone in the community has shared goals, one of which is gaining fluency in the target language. That's why speaking the language and hearing others speak the language is so important. And once we've established a speaking community, we want to add people to it. And today's technologies allow us to do that in ways and on levels, even international levels, like we've never been able to do before.

Another step is to begin creating new resources. And I think this step is at its best when numerous people from within the community are working together, innovating together, and taking risks together to develop these new tools. Leveraging the skills and talents of the community is the way to go! And really it takes a community; community is essential.

Conclusion: And it's my hope that those within this listening community today and perhaps those with ears to hear across the wider global community, would maybe take a greater interest in the languages around them, whether those languages are living, dying, or already dead, and maybe even begin interacting with them. And, so, with that my friends, as we might say in Koine Greek, Εὐχαριστῶ (pronounced: ev-kha-ree-stoh). And if you're not sure what that means, well, as a native Kentuckian, I'm inclined to translate it as, "Thank y'all!"

- What are your initial thoughts about this thesis?

- Go back and look at the 10 traits of a thesis. Are all of them found here?

(15.2) Thesis & Law

Now that you've had an opportunity to analyze a practical (i.e. "political") thesis, it's time to turn your attention to a few related concepts: theoretical thesis, hypothesis, and synthesis. The aim of the theoretical thesis, as the name suggests, is to speak about something theoretical. Examples of this kind of thesis might deal with matters such as whether ghosts exist, what language angels speak, or "whether the sky is spherical, whether there are many worlds, whether the sun is made of fire."[46]

One must be very careful not to confuse theoretical with hypothetical, two terms that, in English, can carry similar meanings or connotations. It might be helpful here to simply begin thinking of the theoretical thesis as a matter relegated to the mind—it's all theory. As found in the text of an ancient orator, one way to think about a hypothesis, however, is simply in contrast to the practical or theoretical thesis: "if we choose a specific person and some circumstance and give an account of reasons in this way, it will be a hypothesis, not a thesis."[47] Thus, a defining difference between the theoretical thesis and the hypothesis has to do with the latter being specific while the former is not.

But there is also synthesis. The philosopher Wilhelm G.W. Hegel greatly popularized this in his thesis-antithesis-synthesis paradigm, his "dialectical" approach, which he developed in the late 1700s to early 1800s. L. Susan Bond describes it this way: "The ideal or sought-after situation is understood as the 'thesis' proposition, that which is to be desired (liberation for the captives). The antithesis is the situation as it really is, less than ideal and fully grounded in the current historical context (more people are in prison than ever before in history)....The synthesis or solution comes about as a result of the 'relevant question,' which identifies the major

---

[46] Kennedy, *Progymnasmata*, 87.

[47] Ibid.

obstacle to realizing the thesis."[48] Sticking with the example of imprisonment, the "relevant question" might be something like the following two inquiries: "Are there government incentives in existence, such as economic benefits, that contribute to and sustain mass incarceration? If so, how might those be addressed and remedied?"

In this lesson, you have two tasks that, comparatively speaking, are pretty easy. The first is to develop three original hypothetical examples. Again, something like "Pope Francis should marry" fits this bill—something both theoretical and specific. Use the entries below to fill in your three examples.

Hypothesis:

Hypothesis:

Hypothesis:

The second is, using a theoretical thesis, to develop three examples of the thesis-antithesis-synthesis model. As with above, use the spaces below and on the next page to fill in the entries.

Thesis:

Antithesis:

Synthesis:

---

[48] L. Susan Bond, *Contemporary African American Preaching: Diversity in Theory and Style* (Danvers, Mass.: Chalice, 2003), 46.

Thesis:

Antithesis:

Synthesis:

Thesis:

Antithesis:

Synthesis:

(15.3) Thesis & Law

As previously promised, in this lesson you are going to be introduced to the progymnasmatic element of law. Right out of the gate, it should be noted that from my perspective, the structure of a law speech or writing should be similar to that of a thesis. Thus, the threefold use of antithesis-solution bracketed between a subtle approach and conclusion should be used.

A difference between thesis and law, however, is that the latter focuses on, well, a law. This law is one that is either currently in place or that has been proposed. The speaker or writer is supposed to attack or defend said law or proposal. Further, as Craig Gibson notes, law "is more complex than a thesis in that a speaker is introduced," yet, it is "less complex than a hypothesis in that it lacks a specific context for the discussion."[49] Sometimes the speaker might be a mythical or historical figure.

As Richard Hidary points out, in Nezikin 5 of the Mekhilta of Rabbi Ishmael, a work in the tradition of ancient Jewish midrash, the law format is used. It follows the antithesis-solution model, although it only does that twice instead of three times. It is bracketed between an opening and concluding remark or, as Hidary labels them, a thesis (statement) and an epilogue.[50] In the example below, I have included the terms I have used right alongside his for the sake of comparison.

Subtle Approach/Thesis: "You shall not steal" [Exod 20:13]: behold this is a warning for the one who kidnaps.

Antithesis 1: You say it is a warning against kidnapping, but perhaps it is only a warning against stealing money?

---

[49] Gibson, *Libanius's* Progymnasmata, 527.

[50] Richard Hidary, *Rabbis and Classical Rhetoric: Sophistic Education and Oratory in the Talmud and Midrash* (Cambridge: Cambridge University Press, 2017), 137-38.

Solution 1: When it states: "You shall not steal, you shall not deal deceitfully or falsely" (Lev 19:11) behold this is a warning against stealing money. What, therefore, does "You shall not steal" (Exod 20:13) teach? This verse is a warning against kidnapping.

Antithesis 2: Or perhaps this verse (Exod 20:13) refers to stealing money and that verse (Lev 19:11) refers to kidnapping?

Solution 2: You should say: three commandments were stated in this context. Two of them are apparent and one is obscure. Let us elucidate the obscure one from the apparent ones. Just as the apparent ones ["You shall not murder" and "You shall not commit adultery"] are commandments for which one is liable to death at the hands of the court, so too the obscure one ["You shall not steal"] is a commandment for which one is liable to death at the hands of the court.

Conclusion/Epilogue: Therefore, you should not say the latter option but rather the former option: this (Exod 20:13) is a warning for kidnapping that (Lev 19:11) is a warning for stealing money.

As you can see, the main law under discussion here by the speaker is Ex 20:13. There is, however, another law that comes into play, namely, Lev 19:11. The speaker argues that Ex 20:13 is a law about "stealing" a person, that is, kidnapping. The line of reason is that it is listed alongside two other laws (i.e. murder in Ex 20:13 and adultery in Ex 20:14) that, if broken, require death. The underlying question is: If two laws require death when they are broken, why wouldn't the third also require it? Since "stealing" say, a piece of fruit, doesn't require the death penalty (see Lev 6:1-7) and one form of stealing (i.e. kidnapping; see Ex 21:16) does, then this must be what that law is referring to—human stealing.

Now that you've had the chance to engage an example of law and see how it is both similar to and different than thesis, take a few moments and jot down a few thoughts about the former. Specifically, write on how thesis and law are alike and different. Use the space below to compose a few thoughts.

(15.4) Thesis & Law

Now it's your turn to compose a piece on law. Use the antithesis-solution formula that you've already seen and which, as you recall, is bracketed between a thesis statement/subtle approach and a conclusion/epilogue. In addition, in this lesson imitate the previous one by drawing on an Old Testament law, specifically, one of the Ten Commandments (see Ex 20:2-17 and/or Dt 5:6-21). (Note: If you really want to imitate the law example in the previous lesson, feel free to use only two antithesis-solution examples. You're welcome!) Use the remainder of this page and the white space on the next to compose.

[Use the blank space below and/or additional paper for composing.]

(15.5) Thesis & Law

Guess what!? This is the last lesson in this book. Once again, I want to congratulate you; you've done well to make it to this point. I sincerely hope you've learned some things and sharpened your reasoning, writing, and creative skills along the way. In this lesson, your task is very simple. As with the previous lesson, you're going to use the antithesis-solution model to compose an argument for or against a law. This law, however, needs to be a modern one. As stated before, it can be one that is currently on the books or is being proposed. Thus, you might have to do a little research to choose one you'd like to write about. As always, feel free to use the white space below and on the next page. Oh, and one last thing, after you compose this law, there's one remaining thing to do: turn to the glossary and define or describe all fourteen elements of the progymnasmata from fable to thesis/law. Didn't see that coming, did you? Have fun!

[Use the blank space below and/or additional paper for composing.]

GLOSSARY & INDEX

Glossary: Terms are Indexed Alphabetically

(Add additional terms at the end of the glossary.)

1 African-Egyptian Orator (8):

2 Semitic Orators (7):

3 Appeals of Rhetoric (23-29):

3 Species of Rhetoric (52-59, 149):

3 Possible Founders of Rhetoric (According to Greek tradition) (12-13):

3 Styles/levels of Speaking (40-41):

5 Canons of Rhetoric (35-51):

5 Virtues of Style (41):

7 Elements of the Rhetorical Triangle (17-29):

Apologia/Apology (55):

Arrangement (37-39):

Audience (18-19):

Chreia (103-14):

Commonplace (149-62):

Comparison (175-90):

[Use the blank space below for additional glossary terms or notes.]

BIBLIOGRAPHY

Bibliography of Modern Sources
(Ancient sources are cited in the body of the book.)

"Basic Questions for Rhetorical Analysis." *Silva Rhetoricae* online. Last accessed February 25, 2018. http://rhetoric.byu.edu/ Pedagogy/ Rhetorical%20Analysis%20heuristic.htm.

Berry, Wendell. "Goforth," in *Jayber Crow: A Novel*. Washington, D.C.: Crosspoint, 2000.

Bond, L. Susan. *Contemporary African American Preaching: Diversity in Theory and Style*. Danvers, Mass.: Chalice, 2003.

Brinsmead, Bernard H. *Galatians: Dialogical Response to Opponents*. SBLDS 65; Chico, Calif.: Scholars, 1982.

Bryan, Stuart and Jared Miller. *Omnibus III: Reformation to the Present*, eds. D. Wilson and G.T. Fischer. Lancaster, PA: Veritas, 2006.

Clifford, Richard J. *Proverbs: A Commentary*. OTL; Louisville: WJK, 1999.

"CNN Transcripts: O.J. Simpson Trial." *CNN* online. Last accessed February 25, 2018. www.cnn.com/US/OJ/ daily/9-28/transcripts/trans5.html.

Colavito, Joseph. "Exordium," in *Encyclopedia of Rhetoric and Composition: Communication from Ancient Times to the Information Age*, ed. T. Enos. GRLH 1389; New York: Routledge, 1996.

Crowley, Sharon and Debra Hawhee, *Ancient Rhetorics for Contemporary Students*. New York: Pearson Longman, 2004.

Dillard, Annie. *Pilgrim at Tinker Creek.* San Francisco: HarperCollins e-books, 2007.

Frobish, Todd S. "An Origin of a Theory: A Comparison of Ethos in the Homeric Iliad with that Found in Aristotle's Rhetoric," *Rhetoric Review* 22/1 (2003): 29.

Gibson, Craig A. *Libanius's Progymnasmata: Model Exercises in Greek Prose Composition and Rhetoric*, ed. M. Heath. WGW 27; Atlanta: Society of Biblical Literature.

Gitay, Yehoshua. "Rhetorical Analysis of Isaiah 40-48: A Study of the Art of Prophetic Persuasion." Ph.D. diss., Emory University, 1978.

Gross, Alan G. and William M. Keith. *Rhetorical Hermeneutics: Invention and Interpretation in the Age of Science.* Albany, N.Y.: State University of New York Press, 1997.

Hartley, John. "Rhetoric," in *Key Concepts in Communication Studies*, 2nd ed., eds. T. O'Sullivan, J. Hartley, D. Saunders, M. Montgomery, and J. Fiske. New York, N.Y.: Routledge, 1994.

"Here are the Most Ridiculous Laws in Every State." *BusinessInsider.com* online. Last accessed October 5, 2017. http://www.businessinsider.com/most-ridiculous-law-in-every-state-2014-2.

Hester, James D. "The Use and Influence of Rhetoric in Galatians 2:1-14," *Theolgische Zeitschrift* 42 (1986): 387-92.

Hidary, *Richard. Rabbis and Classical Rhetoric: Sophistic Education and Oratory in the Talmud and Midrash.* Cambridge: Cambridge University Press, 2017.

Holmes, Jonathan and Adrian Streete. "Introduction," in *Refiguring Mimesis: Representation in Early Modern Literature*, eds. J. Holmes and A. Streete. Hertfordshire: University of Hertfordshire Press, 2005.

Kanahele, George H. and George S. Kanahele, *Ku Kanaka Stand Tall: A Search for Hawaiian Values.* Honolulu: University of Hawaii Press, 1992.

Kennedy, George A. *Progymnasmata: Greek Textbooks of Prose Competition and Rhetoric.* WGW 10; Atlanta: Society of Biblical Literature, 2003.

Keillor, Garrison. "Truckstop," in *Leaving Home.* Place of publication not identified: Penguin Books, 1997.

Long, Fredrick J. *Ancient Rhetoric and Paul's Apology: The Compositional Unity of 2 Corinthians.* SNTSMS 131; Cambridge: Cambridge University Press, 2004.

Matsen, Patricia, Philip Rollins, and Marion Sousa. *Readings from Classical Rhetoric.* Carbondale: Southern Illinois Press, 1990.

McEntyre, Marilyn C. *Caring for Words in a Culture of Lies.* Grand Rapids: Eerdmans, 2009.

McKeown, Richard. "Creativity and the Commonplace," *Philosophy & Rhetoric* 4 (1973): 208.

Moo, Douglas J. "James" in *Hebrews to Revelation*. ZIBBC 4; Grand Rapids: Zondervan, 2002.

Neyrey, Jerome H. "Encomium vs. Vituperation: Contrasting Portraits of Jesus in the Fourth Gospel," in *The Gospel of John in Cultural and Rhetorical Perspective*. Grand Rapids: Eerdmans, 2009.

O'Connor, Flannery. "A View of the Woods," in *Everything that Rises Must Converge*. New York: Farrar, Straus and Giroux, 1993.

Pnella, Robert J. "The Progmynmasmata and Progymnasmatic Theory in Imperial Greek Education," in *A Companion to Ancient Education*, ed. M. Bloomer. Malden, Mass.: John Wiley & Sons, 2015.

Potok, Chaim. *The Gift of Asher Lev*. New York: Fawcett Books, 1997.

Shakespeare, William. *Shakespeare's Sonnets*, ed. K. Duncan-Jones. New York: Bloomsbury, 2016.

Sheldon, H. L. "Some Hawaiian Proverbs," *Hawaiian Almanac and Annual* (1883): 52-58.

Stevenson, Robert Louis. *Strange Case of Dr. Jekyll and Mr. Hyde*. New York: Scriber's Sons, 1886.

Vickers, Brian. *Classical Rhetoric in English Poetry: With a New Preface and Annotated Bibliography*. Carbondale, Southern Illinois University Press, 1989.

Watson, Duane F. "Paul's Rhetorical Strategy in 1 Corinthians 15," in *Rhetoric and the New Testament: Essays from the 1992 Heidelberg Conference*, eds. S.E. Porter and T.H. Olbricht. LNTS; JSNTSS 90; T&T Clark, 2001.

Weaver, William. *Untutored Lines: The Making of the English Epyllion*. Edinburgh: Edinburgh University Press, 2012.

Wiesel, Elie M. *Night*. New York: Hill and Wang, 2006.

Made in United States
North Haven, CT
22 December 2021